DATE DUE

ANCIENT INDIA'S
MYTHS AND BELIEFS

ANCIENT INDIA'S
MYTHS AND BELIEFS

Charles Phillips, Michael Kerrigan, and David Gould

ROSEN
PUBLISHING®

New York

This edition published in 2012 by:

The Rosen Publishing Group, Inc.
29 East 21st Street
New York, NY 10010

Additional end matter copyright © 2012 by The Rosen Publishing Group, Inc.

Library of Congress Cataloging-in-Publication Data

Phillips, Charles.
Ancient India's myths and beliefs/Charles Phillips, Michael Kerrigan, David Gould.
     p. cm.—(World mythologies)
Includes bibliographical references (p.   ) and index.
ISBN 978-1-4488-5990-0 (library binding)
1. Mythology, Indic. 2. Hindu mythology. 3. India—Religion. I. Kerrigan, Michael, 1959– II. Gould, David. III. Title.
BL2001.3.P55 2012
294.5'13—dc23

2011036650

Manufactured in the United States of America

CPSIA Compliance Information: Batch #W12YA: For further information, contact Rosen Publishing, New York, New York, at 1-800-237-9932.

Series copyright © 1998 Time-Life Books
Text copyright © 1998 Duncan Baird Publishers
Commissioned illustrations copyright © 1998 Brent Hardy-Smith

Photo Credits:

The publisher would like to thank the following people, museums and photographic libraries for permission to reproduce their material. Every care has been taken to trace copyright holders. However, if we have omitted anyone we apologize and will, if informed, make corrections in any future edition.

Key:
t top; c center; b bottom; l left; r right

Abbreviations:

BM	British Museum, London	NMI	National Museum of India, New Delhi
BAL	Bridgeman Art Library	V&A	Victoria and Albert Museum, London
ET	ET Archive	WFA	Werner Forman Archive
RHPL	Robert Harding Picture Library		

Title page: BAL/V&A; **Contents page:** V&A; **6** RHPL/JHC Wilson; **7** RHPL/A Kennet; **8** RHPL/P Koch; **10** BAL/NMI; **11** RHPL/JHC Wilson; **12** BL; **13** Christie's Images; **14t** Christie's Images; **14c** RHPL; **14b** RHPL; **15l** BAL/NMI; **15bc** Christie's Images; **15r** Magnum/Henri Cartier-Bresson; **16** Getty Images/Paul Harris; **17** ET/BL; **18–19** RHPL/Jeremy Bright; **20** RHPL/Gavin Hellier; **21** Chester Beatty Library, Dublin; **22** BL; **23** RHPL/JHC Wilson; **24t** Chris Caldicott; **24b** Chris Caldicott; **24–25** Getty Images/Mike McQueen; **25t** Getty Images/Mike McQueen; **25b** RHPL; **26** V&A; **27** Images Colour Library; **28** Christie's Images; **31** Michael Holford; **32** V&A; **33** BAL/V&A; **35** V&A; **36** BAL/NMI; **37** V&A; **38** V&A; **39r** BAL/V&A; **39tl** BAL/V&A; **39r** V&A; **40tl** BAL/Dinodia, Bombay; **40–41** V&A; **41** Ann & Bury Peerless; **42** V&A; **43** BAL/Oriental Museum, Durham University; **44** V&A; **45** V&A; **46** John Cleare; **47** V&A; **48** Chris Caldicott; **50** V&A; **51** John Cleare; **52** BAL/NMI; **52–53** Chris Caldicott; **53** Chris Caldicott; **54** Getty Images/David Sutherland; **55t** RHPL; **55c** Panos Pictures/Jeremy Horner; **55b** RHPL/JHC Wilson; **56** BAL/V&A; **57** NMI; **58** Michael Holford/Horniman Museum; **59** ET/V&A; **60** V&A; **61** BAL/NMI; **62** WFA/V&A; **63** Christie's Images; **64** BAL/NMI; **65** V&A; **66** V&A; **68** BAL/Dinodia, Bombay; **69** Images Colour Library; **70** Christie's Images; **72** BAL/V&A; **73** BAL; **75** V&A; **76** WFA/Philip Goldman Collection; **77** BAL/NMI; **78** BL; **79** RHPL/Maurice Joseph; **80–81** V&A; **84** BL; **85** Christie's Images; **86–87** V&A; **88** Christie's Images; **90** BAL/V&A; **91tl** Panos Pictures/Sareta & Jules Cowan; **91tc** Panos Pictures/JC Callow; **91tr** Getty Images/Grilly Bernard; **91cl** RHPL/JHC Wilson; **91c** Panos Pictures/Neil Cooper; **91cr** RHPL/JHC Wilson; **91bl** RHPL/JHC Wilson; **91bc** Getty Images/Hilarie Kavanagh; **91br** RHPL/JHC Wilson; **92** V&A; **93** BM; **94** Christies; **95** BAL/NMI; **96** V&A; **97** Getty Images/Ben Edwards; **98–99** BAL/NMI; **100** Michael Holford/V&A; **101** Hutchison; **102** V&A/M Kitcatt; **104** Christies Images; **105** BAL/V&A; **106–7** BAL/NMI; **107** RHPL/Tony Gervis; **108** Images; **109** ET/V&A; **112-3** BL; **112t** RHPL/Adam Woolfitt; **113cr** V&A; **114tl** RHPL/F Salviati; **114bl** Madhu Khana, New Delhi; **114tr** V&A/M Kitcatt; **114br** BL; **115** Pepita Seth, New Delhi; **116t** BAL/NMI; **117** WFA/Private Collection; **118** RHPL/Nigel Blythe; **119** RHPL/JamesGreen; **120** BAL/BM; **122** RHPL/Alison Wright; **123** Peerless; **124** Panos Pictures/Cliff Venner; **126** Christie's Images; **127** BAL; **128** RHPL; **130** Axiom/Neil Barclay; **131** Christie's Images; **132** V&A; **133** WFA/Private Collection; **135** Ronald Grant Archive/Doordarshan/BBC; **136** RHPL/G Corrigan; **137** Hyphen Films/Basant Studio

Contents

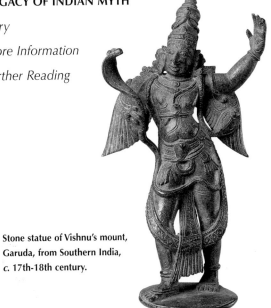

Stone statue of Vishnu's mount, Garuda, from Southern India, *c.* 17th-18th century.

A SACRED HISTORY

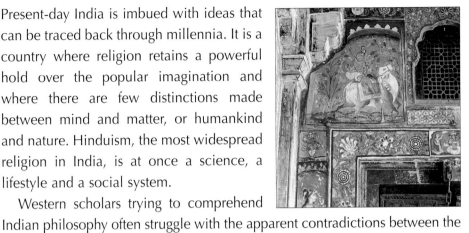

Present-day India is imbued with ideas that can be traced back through millennia. It is a country where religion retains a powerful hold over the popular imagination and where there are few distinctions made between mind and matter, or humankind and nature. Hinduism, the most widespread religion in India, is at once a science, a lifestyle and a social system.

Western scholars trying to comprehend Indian philosophy often struggle with the apparent contradictions between the different schools of thought and the obscure terminology of the key texts—many of which were written for aesthetic or symbolic, rather than didactic, effect. But the key to understanding them lies not in logic but in the Indian convention of *vidya* (unitary thought), which seeks to understand phenomena as a single system, in which God and Man are one and enlightenment lies in realizing infinite harmony with the universe. As one of the *Upanishads* expresses it: *atman* (the vital force in all things) is *brahman* (absolute truth).

The study of Indian history is complicated by other aspects of the culture's way of thinking: *karma* and *samsara*, the cycles of causality and rebirth. We are all rewarded or punished for our deeds, and reincarnated in a new form—as an animal, perhaps, or as a member of a different caste. This idea of non-linear time, in which past, present and future coexist in each generation, made the keeping of historical records seem irrelevant until very recently.

The diversity of India's culture means that generalizations count for little. Its population includes tribespeople, peasants and holy men whose lives have remained unchanged through generations, and wealthy capitalists, movie moguls and Nobel-prize-winning scientists who have thrived amid the advance of technology. India contains massive urban conglomerations, deserts, mountains, forests, croplands and the mighty rivers—the Indus, Ganges, Yamuna, and Tungabhadra. There are seven major religions (Hinduism, Buddhism, Jainism, Sikhism, Islam, Christianity and Zoroastrianism), fourteen official languages and 1,652 recognized dialects. And, unlike the mythology of Greece or Rome, India's legends remain at the center of daily life, a continuing part of the tapestry of modern India.

Above: Shiva is at once protector and destroyer, dancer and ascetic. Here he rides his faithful bull Nandi in a temple mural from Bundi, near Ajmer.

Opposite: The Jain temple complex at Junagadh looks out across the Gujarat plains. Such sites offer a focus that is as much social and cultural as spiritual.

The Riches of the Indus

Humans first set foot in the vast Indian subcontinent between 400,000 BCE and 200,000 BCE. The archaeological evidence is sketchy, but it appears that one wave of migrants moved east and south from present-day Afghanistan and Tadjikistan into what is now Pakistan. In the same period, other peoples may have sailed to southern India from the east coast of Africa, establishing a culture very different from that which developed in the north.

For thousands of millennia the early Indians left little trace of their culture and lifestyle, but around 2500 BCE a more advanced and settled civilization began to emerge in the valley of the Indus, in what is now Pakistan. The Indus Valley civilization eventually reached into the Punjab, Sind, Rajasthan, Delhi and as far west as Kathiawar, covering more than 386,100 square miles (more than a million square kilometers). There is evidence that these people traded with the great powers of Egypt and Sumeria. Their writing remains undeciphered, so our knowledge of this culture is based mainly on the archaeological clues provided by two of more than seventy urban excavations: Harappa, in the Punjab, and Mohenjo-Daro, 186 miles (300 kilometers) northeast of Karachi, on the Indus.

These two cities, protected by thick adobe walls and laid out in a grid pattern, suggesting there was a strong central planning authority, are distinguished by their prominent citadels, communal granaries, excellent water supplies and carefully engineered brick sewers to carry away waste. At Mohenjo-Daro, the remains of a large bitumen-lined bath in what appears to be a temple or priestly residence has inspired much speculation, for it appears to prefigure the ritual bathing tanks that still form part of Hindu temples.

The ruins of a Buddhist citadel among the crumbling adobe walls of Mohenjo-Daro. Covering some 741 acres (300 hectares), it was once one of the largest Bronze Age cities in the world.

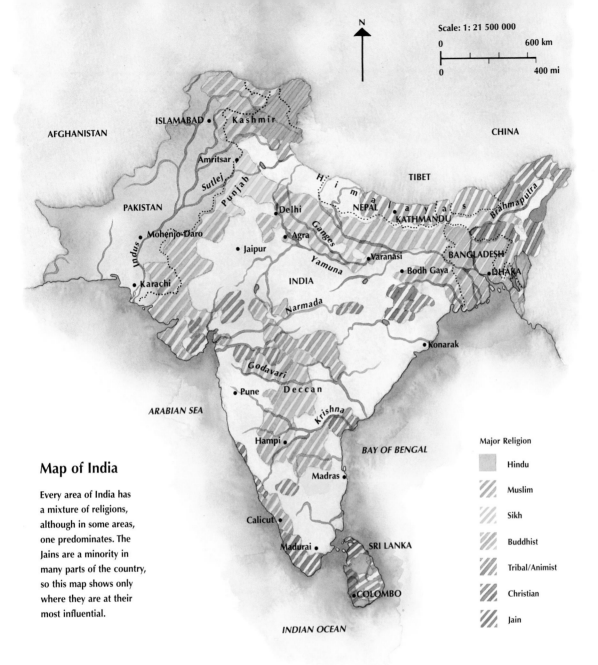

Map of India

Every area of India has
a mixture of religions,
although in some areas,
one predominates. The
Jains are a minority in
many parts of the country,
so this map shows only
where they are at their
most influential.

Major Religion

Hindu

Muslim

Sikh

Buddhist

Tribal/Animist

Christian

Jain

The most puzzling Indus artifacts, however, are the small, square seals made of steatite, a soap-stone. Scratched with undeciphered pictograms, they depict an enormous variety of animals: rhinoceroses, elephants, tigers, snakes, crocodiles, antelopes, zebu and goats, but most frequently a single-horned bull with a short, stylized post in front of it. The significance of this icon has remained a mystery. Is it an image of phallus worship that prefigured the cult of the *lingam* in later Hinduism, an animal before a sacrificial altar, or simply a farm beast standing at a manger?

One seal is particularly intriguing: it depicts a masked, horned male figure clad in tiger skin, seated in a yogic posture and surrounded by wild beasts. It is thought to be an early depiction of the god Shiva. Another shows a god emerging from a tree, with a bull and dancing girls in attendance. This deity is depicted with three horns, and scholars have suggested that these could prefigure Shiva's trident. Together, these images suggest that both Shiva and his companion and steed, the sacred bull Nandi, may have their origins deep in the shadowy past of the Indus civilization.

9

Indus culture started to decline around 1750 BCE. There seem to have been several reasons for this, not least because the Indus civilization was so far-flung: conditions in the Rajasthan desert differed greatly from those at the coast or in the foothills of the Himalayas. Geological change (a rapid rise in sea level, the silting up of several key rivers and a rerouting of the Indus itself) may have fatally damaged trade; Mohenjo-Daro and Harappa were battered by repeated floods; and there is evidence that waves of attacks by more primitive invaders brought chaos and panic. Fire damage and groups of huddled corpses in the streets of Mohenjo-Daro suggest that this city underwent a final cataclysm—perhaps an earthquake or an invasion.

The Aryan Invasion

There was an interlude of 200–300 years between the end of the Indus civilization and the invasion of seminomadic Aryan tribes that for many historians marks the beginning of the story of India. The Aryans appear to have fled their homeland between the Caspian and Black seas in around 2000 BCE, dispersing in all directions; England, Ireland, Greece, Rome, Germany and Iran all bear traces of Aryan settlement. It was Iranian Aryans who, in around 1500 BCE, crossed the Hindu Kush mountains to settle in the Indus Valley.

The early Aryans left no archaeological traces, so what we know of them comes from the *Vedas* ("books of knowledge")— religious texts based on a rich oral tradition. They appear to have been a hearty, lusty race, frequently indulging in wine, gambling, music and fighting. The *Vedas* describe how these warlike, pale-skinned, cattle-herding people, mounted on horseback, soon subdued and enslaved the Dasas, who had populated the Indus Valley before them.

The Aryans brought several traditions that still hold sway in India. They herded their cherished cattle into India, and they brought with them a love of dairy produce and a grave reverence for the animal itself: beef was permitted only on special occasions. They also introduced a social structure that anticipated the caste system. To their traditional class division of *kshatriya* (warrior aristocracy), *brahmin* (priests) and *vaishya* (farmers and traders), they added at the very bottom *shudra* (dark-skinned pre-Aryan people).

Over the 500 years or so of Aryan dominance in northern India, religion changed from the worship of simple nature gods to a cosmic pantheon of thirty-three gods, including Indra, Agni and Soma, gods who would find a place in later religions. Indra is reminiscent of the Viking war god Thor, destroying his demonic rival Vritra with thunderbolts and freeing light, water and cattle that were trapped in darkness. Agni, the god of fire and the sun, received offerings through smoke, while Soma was celebrated through the hallucinogenic plant that brought visions of immortality to those who drank its elixir.

Gradually, as the Aryans spread eastward along the Ganges Valley, their political, social, religious and cultural traditions were suffused with local

A terracotta mother goddess from Mohenjo-Daro, *c.* 2300–1750 BCE. The many female gods of later Hindu imagery are believed to have derived from the once widespread worship of a single all-encompassing female deity.

Holy Men

India's sadhus *reflect a tradition that goes back to the very dawn of Indian culture, their lifestyle shaped by the belief that god can be found only through self-denial.*

Austerity is a theme that recurs throughout the ancient Vedic and Brahmanic texts. Self-denial and even self-torture, it is asserted, help to win a higher place in the afterlife. India's *sadhus*, or holy men, aim to attain nirvana (extinction of being) and *moksha* (release from the cycle of rebirth) by a life of self-denial and prayer.

Retreat, celibacy, poverty and vegetarianism are essential milestones on the road to holiness. Some *sadhus* become hermits and spend their lives in a cave, a tree or a forest clearing, meditating on the nature of god and being. Others take up residence in temples, and many become

monks who wander across the country, their lives continuous pilgrimages from one site to another.

Many choose to follow Shiva, and they carry tridents and various other symbols of the god. Others go naked except for a dusting of ashes. Individual *sadhus* choose their

A *sadhu* meditates, smeared in ashes that reflect his religious conviction.

own form of expression, and spend their lives sleeping with venomous snakes, holding one arm up in the air or standing on one leg, wearing spiked sandals or hanging upside down.

pre-Aryan customs. They learned the Indus art of building towns, lost the nomadic habit and settled in village communities. By 1000 BCE the first Indian kingdoms had emerged in the Ganges and Indus valleys, the story of which is told with lavish helpings of fantasy in the two great early Sanskrit epics called the *Mahabharata* ("Great Bharata") and the *Ramayana* ("Story of Rama").

Meanwhile, the south of the Indian subcontinent remained relatively unchanged. Some people continued to live as Stone Age tribes, although iron started to appear in various locations between 500 CE and 1000 CE. The culture in Assam suggests connections with China, while a sophisticated literary culture flourished in Tamil from about 100 CE. In

the southern tip, between 1000 BCE and the first century CE, people of the Megalithic culture erected dolmens, menhirs and stone circles, apparently in connection with ancestor worship. The reluctance, or inability, of Ganges Valley dwellers to take the road south has left a lasting linguistic legacy, for southern Indians today speak Dravidian rather than the Indo-Aryan languages of the north.

As Aryan culture made its mark, the foundations of practical Hinduism were being laid down. Over the centuries, different schools of priests emerged around each of the four *samhitas* (collections) of *Vedas*: the *Rig Veda* spawned the *hotr*, priests who specialized in pouring oblations; the *Sama Veda* inspired *udgatr* priests, who chanted

Hinduism's Principal Texts

The five essential texts of Hinduism, in which the great Hindu myths are recounted, have evolved over nearly 3,000 years and contain stories that are still recited and performed throughout India today.

The *Rig Veda*, composed around 1000 BCE, is a collection of hymns to the gods that have been sung by generations of priestly families. The *Brahmanas* were composed by *brahmin* priests in about 800 BCE. They are the first layer of commentaries on the *Vedas*, and expand on the significance and detail of sacred rituals.

The *Mahabharata* was compiled by poets and priests between 300 BCE and 300 CE. It tells the story of an epic struggle for power between Aryan kings in the first millennium BCE. It also contains the *Bhagavad Gita* ("Lord's Song"), the tenets of Hinduism as related by Krishna.

The *Ramayana* ("Story of Rama") is another royal epic, set in Ayodhya in about 800 BCE. Its author, Valmiki (writing at least 500 years later), relates the efforts of King Rama, an incarnation of Vishnu, to claim his throne, and gives a dramatic and colorful account of the great myths.

The *Puranas* are a collection of instructions and stories compiled between 500 BCE and 1000 CE. Today's versions of the Hindu myths are mainly derived from this easily digestible source.

A page from a 15th-century copy of the *Rig Veda*, the text that defined what became known as the Vedic age.

mantras; and the sacrificial formulas of the *Yajur Vedas* gave rise to *adhvaryu*, priests who acted as overall masters of ceremony, making sure temple services were run properly. The *brahmins*, priests associated with the *Atharva Veda*—a sage's gloss on the other three *Vedas*—gained ascendancy as a class of superior priests who oversaw the activities of the other three groups.

By 700 BCE, priests had established an iron grip on all aspects of religious life, and even kings acknowledged their supremacy as divine representatives on Earth. The priests compiled lengthy commentaries on the *Vedas,* which added extra layers to the already elaborate theology of Brahmanism. The *Brahmanas,* which because of their dense prose and elusive meaning lack the drama of many other Vedic texts, set out the meaning and proce-dure of the religious rituals. The *Aranyakas* (forest texts) offer further explanations and allegories, and the *Upanishads* are mystical reflections on the nature of the universe and its relation to *brahman*, the "absolute truth" that governs it. The *Upan-ishads* became the basis of the most important school in Hindu philosophy, known as the *Vedanta*.

By around 600 BCE, the Ganges Valley was occupied by a string of hereditary monarchies whose agricultural wealth led them to trade, and sometimes fight, with each other. New towns such as Kashi (modern Varanasi), Ayodhya and Shravasti sprang up along the main trading routes, and they displayed all the trappings of a sophisticated urban economy: coinage, private property, guilds, banks and a common script called Brahmi.

The situation in the Punjab and the Himalayan foothills, by contrast, was republican. Tribes or groups of local tribes were ruled by an elected chief, supported by councils of elders. Drums summoned all to general assemblies at which key decisions were debated and agreed.

The relative prosperity of the kingdoms gave some people the leisure to pursue philosophical interests, and trade brought many different influences into the area. The republics' practice of open debate also encouraged religious speculation. Both factors helped to support the rise of alternative religions in the sixth century BCE, the most important of which was to be Buddhism.

Buddhism and Jainism

Siddhartha Gautama, the Buddha (enlightened one), lived in northern India from about 560 to about 480 BCE. The son of a nobleman, he embarked on a quest for spiritual enlightenment at the age of twenty-nine. His core teaching became known as the Four Noble Truths. In summary, the Buddha said that the universe is a place of suffering and pain, caused by a complex chain of causation that manifests itself as desire. We are doomed to experience *samsara* (rebirth)—a concept shared by Hinduism—and a continuation of suffering unless we break the cycle by practicing the Eightfold Path of right views, right intention, right speech, right conduct, right livelihood, right effort, right mindfulness, and right concentration. Once this has been achieved, we are said to reach the ultimate state of nirvana.

In the centuries after the Buddha's death, his ideas were developed further by his followers into a complex system. Buddhism's strong monastic tradition dates from this period, when wandering monks and nuns began to collect and preserve the lessons of their master. His teachings are still followed by millions of Buddhists throughout Asia and in the West. Although Buddhism is now growing in India, it is no longer an important part of India's religious makeup.

Less popular today, but immensely influential nonetheless, is Jainism, which has nearly four million adherents, mainly in western India. The creed was based on ideas that were already in circulation but were given form by Mahavira, a contemporary

This sculpture, from Gandhara, *c.* 2nd century CE, shows the Buddha in familiar meditative pose. While forging a separate spiritual tradition, Buddhism also had a great influence on Hinduism.

13

of the Buddha, and like him, an ascetic who left home in the quest for enlightenment. Jains do not believe in the power of deities, but they think that every living thing houses an immortal soul. Observant Jains are strict vegetarians and often take extreme measures to avoid injuring anything—even accidentally. Monks wear face masks so they do not breathe in tiny insects, and pilgrims sweep the road ahead so as not to tread on ants or other creatures. Through celibacy, fasting, poverty and other ascetic practices, Jains hope to achieve the purification of the soul, which they believe is the ultimate purpose

This 10th-century sandstone head represents a *tirthankara*, one of the builders of bridges between life and death. Mahavira, the founder of Jainism, was the 24th, and final, *tirthankara*.

of life on Earth.

In the fifth century BCE, the kings of Magadha conquered several of their rivals to emerge as the major political force in the Ganges Valley. From their capital at Rajagriha in northeastern India, a series of ambitious rulers created a rich, well-run and stable nation. After the death of Ajatashatru (491–461 BCE), however, Magadha underwent a decline until some time after 362 BCE, when Mahapadma Nanda, a barber's son, usurped the throne. News of the power of the Nandas spread even to Greece, and the size of the Magadhan army may have been why Alexander the Great's

TIMELINE	400,000–1500 BCE	1500–1000 BCE	1000–200 BCE

The history of India is one marked by dynastic rivalry interspersed with long periods of alien occupation. All those who sought to conquer or unify the subcontinent, from the Aryans and Greeks, to the Islamic Mughals and the Christian British have left their particular cultural mark on the country's physical and spiritual landscape.

c. 400,000–200,000 The first people begin to roam the plains of the Indian subcontinent.
c. 10,000 Settlements become established throughout southern India.
c. 7000 Early agricultural methods spread across northern India.
c. 4000 Settlements in the Indus Valley cohere toward the first great Indian civilization. Bronze and copper working becomes widespread.
c. 2500 The Indus Valley civilization is at its height.
c. 2000 The Aryan peoples spread out in all directions from their homeland near the Caspian Sea.
c. 1750 The cultures of the Indus Valley begin their decline.

Above and left: A horse and ox decorate stone seals from Mohenjo-Daro, c. 2300–1750 BCE.

1500 Vedic Aryans, from Iran and Afghanistan, cross the Hindu Kush into the Indus Valley. Emergence of Brahmins and Hinduism; composition of the *Rig Veda*.
c. 1200 Shift from pastoral nomadism to more settled agriculture along the Ganges.

c. 1000 Indian kingdoms spring up along the Ganges.
c. 800 Composition of *Brahmanas* secures priests' social dominance. Beginning of the compilation of the *Mahabharata*.
c. 540 Ascendancy of the kings of Magadha in the Ganges Valley.
527 Death of Mahavira, father of Jainism.
528–461 Life of Siddhartha Gautama, founder of Buddhism.
c. 500 *Puranas* and *Upanishads* begin to be collected.
327–325 Alexander the Great invades northwest India.
c. 300 Spread of Buddhism. Building of Amaravati. Valmiki compiles the epic poem, the *Ramayana*.
272–232 Rule of Ashoka, who embraces Buddhist teaching.
c. 200 Waves of invaders fragment India into small principalities.

invasion of India in 327 BCE stopped in the Punjab.

Although Alexander left behind an occupying force, his withdrawal created instability and a power vacuum in the northwest of India. Such political opportunities were exploited by the Magadhan king Chandragupta Maurya (321–297 BCE). Weakened kingdoms and republics were added to Chandragupta's kingdom as he made his way towards the Indus, where the Greek Seleucids, Alexander's successors, put up a stiff resistance before eventually falling in 303 BCE.

Chandragupta's successors built on his achievement, creating an empire that covered southern Afghanistan and the entire Indian subcontinent except the extreme south. The most remarkable Mauryan emperor, Ashoka (272–232 BCE), left edicts carved on stones and on decorated polished stone pillars, which can still be seen today. Ashoka was an enlightened ruler who put the welfare of his subjects first, planting trees along roadsides for shade, digging wells, and setting up a network of hostels for travellers. He embraced Buddhism and urged his subjects to follow the Buddhist principles of *dharma*, a code of conduct that urged respect for other people and nonviolence. The emperor even sent special *dharma* officers to explain this philosophy to people in all corners of his empire.

The strong, centralized administration created by Ashoka soon collapsed after his death and the empire began to break up under the pressure of invasions from Bactrian Greeks, Scythians and central Asian nomadic peoples. From about 200 BCE to about 300 CE India was fragmented into smaller principalities once again. Trade, however, continued to grow vigorously. In addition to the goods that moved along the great trade routes to China, Cambodia and beyond, there also travelled the

200 BCE–400 CE	400–1500	1500–1900	1900 to the present day

A scene from the Ramayana, written by Valmiki around 300 BCE.

c. 100 Trade between Rome and northern India is at its height.
c. 200 Gandharan Buddhist art develops its distinctive style.
c. 320 The Gupta dynasty is established by Chandragupta.
c. 400 Hinduism flourishes under the Gupta dynasty, along with its art and literature.

c. 500 Hun invaders begin to harass the Gupta empire.
c. 650 India begins a return to regionalism and local cultures.
971 The Afghan ruler Mahmud of Ghazni declares a holy war against India, aiming to conquer it in the name of Islam.
1001 The raids of Mahmud of Ghazni begin, destroying Somnath and leading to the occupation of the Punjab, in northern India.
c. 1100 The Vaishnava movement emerges, championing the worship of Vishnu as principal Hindu god.
1192 The Muslim occupation spreads quickly throughout northern and eastern India.
c. 1200 The temple complexes at Konarak are built.
1206 The influential Sultanate is established in Delhi.
1398 Delhi is sacked by the Mongol leader, Timur.
1498 The Portuguese arrive in Calicut, and become the first Europeans in the subcontinent.

1526 Babur founds the Mughal dynasty and aims to unite India.
1538 Guru Nanak, the founder of Sikhism, dies.
1610 The Dutch arrive in India.
1612 The British set up trading posts along the Indian coast.
1658 Aurangzeb ends age of religious tolerance by destroying Hindu temples.
1757 Clive's victory at Plassey brings Bengal under British rule.
1857 Indian "mutiny" begins push for independence.
1885 The Indian National Congress is established.

A 17th-century Mughal jade-hilted dagger. Northern India.

1906 The all-India Muslim League is established, laying the foundations for the split between India's Hindus and Muslims.
1919 British soldiers massacre Indian civilians at Amritsar.
1920 Mohandas Gandhi takes control of the Indian National Congress.
1940 Jinnah proposes the Muslim state of Pakistan.
1947 The British hand over power to the governments of India and Pakistan.
1948 Gandhi is assassinated.
1971 East Pakistan becomes Bangladesh.

Mohandas Gandhi, who led India to independence, only to be assassinated the following year.

powerful spiritual concepts of Buddhism.

The coming of Chandragupta I (320–335 CE) marks the beginning of India's "classical age"—a time during which the arts, science, literature and philosophy flourished. Through astute marriages, political cunning and brute force, Chandragupta and his successors, the Gupta dynasty, subdued a vast area that stretched from the Himalayas to the Deccan and from Karachi to Dhaka.

It was under the Guptas that the key tenets of modern Hinduism began to emerge. The practice of

The 11th-century Sas Bahu temple, near Udaipur in Rajasthan, displays the features of many Hindu places of worship. Its open courtyard contains several shrines to different gods.

image worship became established, and with it the shape of the Hindu temple, with its enclosed courtyard and shrine room containing an image of a god. Major philosophies, including *Vedanta* and Yoga, emerged, and many important texts, including the *Puranas* and the *Kama Sutra*, were composed. The plays of the great Sanskrit author Kalidasa, whose masterpiece, *Shakuntala*, greatly influenced the German playwright Goethe, were also written under Gupta patronage. An even wider impact was made by advances in science and mathematics. The decimal system and Arabic numerals both originated in India, and they were used by astronomers such as Aryabhata, who in the sixth century calculated with precision both the length of a solar year and the precise value of π.

From the fifth century, the Gupta empire was increasingly battered by waves of marauding Hunas (Huns) from Mongolia. The persistent disruption caused the Gupta kingdom to disintegrate into four areas ruled by different dynasties. India's story from 650 CE to the Afghan invasions of the eleventh century is one of regionalism and the increasing development of local cultures.

With the rise of the Pallava and Pandya dynasties in Tamil Nadu, the focus for historians of Indian culture moves southward. Strong leaders such as Nandivarman II (730–796) and Shrimara Shrivallabha (815–862) helped to introduce Indo-Aryan customs such as Brahmanism and Sanskrit writing into the traditional Dravidian culture of Tamil Nadu, Kerala and beyond. Magnificent temples in the Dravidian architectural style, such as the Minakshi at Madurai and Shrirangam (near Trichinopoly) are proof of the successful blending of southern and northern traditions.

In 711, the Arab general Muhammad ibn Qasim conquered Sind, and its inhabitants rapidly converted to Islam. Sind, however, remained an isolated province of the Arab caliphate. In the early eleventh century, the Afghan ruler Mahmud of Ghazni (971–1030) began a holy war to conquer the whole of India in the name of Islam. He led more than twenty campaigns in northern India, opening up a pathway for Afghans, Turks and

Persians to enter the subcontinent.

The Afghan Ghurid caliphs followed in Mahmud's footsteps. In 1193 their formidable armies conquered Delhi, and a long period of aggressive Muslim occupation, known as the Delhi Sultanate, began. The sultanate reached its peak under Ala ud-Din (1296–1316), who conquered large areas of southern India before Mongol invasions forced the sultans to concentrate their forces in the north. The south regained its independence, and in 1398 the Mongol leader Timur sacked Delhi and reduced the sultanate's power, making it just one of a number of Muslim-ruled states in the north. Any hopes of large-scale conversion to Islam were dashed as it became clear that local people remained loyal to the Hindu gods.

The Rise of the Mughals

In 1526 the Afghan ruler Babur (1483–1530), a direct descendant of Genghis Khan (1160–1227) and Timur, defeated the sultan, captured Delhi and conquered a large swathe of territory to found the remarkable Mughal dynasty. Under his son Humayun (1508–1556), Mughal dominance of northern India was defended from repeated Afghan and Hindu challenges. Humayun's son Akbar (1542–1605) was one of the most enlightened and successful rulers India has ever had.

Akbar's main policy was to unite India under Mughal rule, and by 1600 he had conquered land that stretched from Gujarat to Bengal, and Kabul to Kashmir. He was a shrewd conciliator, bringing Hindu rulers into his administration, promoting Din-e Ilahi, a religious system that blended Zoroastrianism, Islam and Hinduism, and even opening his court to Western influences: Jain and Jesuit missions visited on several occasions. Under Akbar a stable, fair administration developed, the judiciary was reformed and the arts flourished.

Akbar's son Jahangir (1569–1627) and grandson Shah Jahan (1592–1666) presided over a golden age of prosperity and political stability, nurturing a remarkable artistic renaissance. Jahangir's success in battle (completing the conquest of the

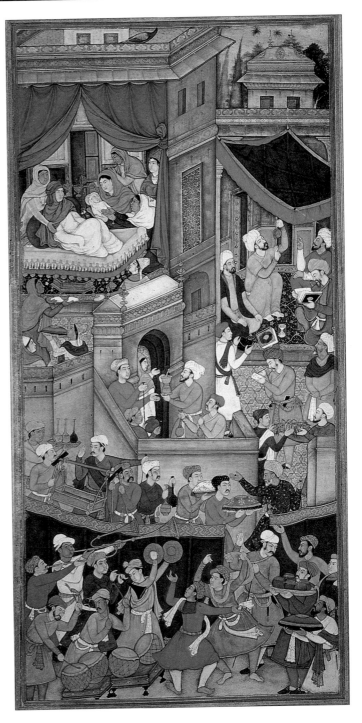

Astrologers cast horoscopes during celebrations of the birth of Timur, from the Mughal text, the *Akbarnameh*. Timur, feared and renowned in the West as Tamerlane, was famed in India for sacking Delhi and ending the rule of the sultanate that had vigorously tried to impose Islam on the city's Hindu population.

17

Disciples of a Single God

India's youngest religion was founded by Guru Nanak, who rejected both Hinduism and Islam to find a path of his own.

"There is no Hindu. There is no Muslim. There is only One who is the creator and uncaused cause of all. God is One. Guru Nanak." So say the followers of the man who founded Sikhism, who lived from 1469 to 1539. He was succeeded by nine other gurus, the last of whom died in 1708. Especially strong in the Punjab and in Himachal Pradesh, Sikhs (the word means "disciples") learned to be a martial people in the course of centuries of persecution.

Sikhs, identifiable throughout the world by their turbans and beards, do not smoke or drink.

They wear the five Ks: *kesh* (long hair), *kangha* (a comb in the hair), *kara* (a bracelet), *kachha* (shorts) and *kirpan* (a sword).

There are some 17 million Sikhs in India today, but they continue to campaign for their own homeland.

The Sikhs' holiest site is the Golden Temple at Amritsar, built in 1604.

Deccan) was counterbalanced by his love of drink and opium. He was a ruthless and cruel ruler: he blinded his rebellious son Khusraw and killed Khusraw's supporter Guru Arjun, opening a schism with India's Sikhs that still surfaces in contemporary Indian politics. Fortunately, Jahangir left the day-to-day running of the empire to his fairer-minded Persian-born wife, Nur Jahan.

In typical Mughal style, Shah Jahan started his political career by rising up against his father. In 1623, disgruntled by Nur Jahan's championing of a rival for the succession, he attempted to capture a series of key towns, but was crushed by the emperor's forces. He eventually ensured his succession by murdering his brothers and all other potential rivals. On becoming emperor he captured Kandahar and in 1646 expanded his empire into northern Afghanistan. He made Delhi his capital, and although Muslim himself, he tolerated Hinduism. Shah Jahan's lasting memorial takes the form of buildings: two magnificent halls in Delhi, the Diwan-i Am and the Diwan-i Kas; and two great masterpieces of Mughal architecture in Agra, the Pearl Mosque and the Taj Mahal, a spectacular

The Taj Mahal in Agra is one of the most celebrated buildings in the world. Built by Shah Jahan to commemorate his wife Mumtaz Mahal, who had died giving birth to their 14th child, it embodies his belief that life is short but love is eternal.

monument to his favorite wife Mumtaz Mahal.

Shah Jahan's reign ended abruptly in 1658, when his son Aurangzeb (1618–1707)—having first taken the usual precaution of murdering and incarcerating his brothers—imprisoned him in the Agra fort. He abandoned the policy of religious tolerance, imposing Islamic law on his empire, destroying thousands of Hindu temples, discriminating against Hindus and Sikhs and forcibly converting many non-believers. Rebellions, all of which were put down with extreme ruthlessness, followed in Mathura, the Punjab and Jodhpur.

Aurangzeb expanded the empire, annexing the Hindu kingdoms of Bijapur and Golconda in 1686–1687. However, he became bogged down in an expensive struggle with the Hindu Maratha kings in Maharashtra, east of Bombay, a dynasty founded by Shivaji (1627–1680) and at this time a powerful force. Aurangzeb's enthusiasm for campaigning meant long absences from court, weakening both his power and the empire. After his death, a series of short-lived emperors failed to overcome endemic factionalism. The sacking of Delhi in 1739 by the Persian invader Nadir Shah sealed the fate of Mughal power.

The Arrival of the Europeans

Meanwhile, progress in navigation, trade and imperial policy in Europe led to an increasing impact on India's economy and politics. In 1498 Portuguese navigator Vasco da Gama landed in Calicut, opening up an era of frequent visits from Europe's great powers. Portugal's subsequent attempts to colonize southern India failed, although it established a thriving trading post at Goa. The Dutch East India Company (founded in 1602) established a tenuous economic foothold in India, but its main emphasis was further east and south, in Indonesia. Its British counterpart, on the other hand, created thriving "factories" (fortified trading posts) at Madras (1639), Bombay (1668) and Calcutta (1690). France, too, had interests in the area, with bases on the islands of Reunion and Mauritius and in Pondicherry on the mainland.

As India's emerging powers—the *peshwas* of Pune, the Nizam of Hyderabad and the *nawabs* of Oudh, Bengal and beyond—jockeyed for supremacy, the British and French East India companies expanded their own commercial and political influence. Exploiting local feuds, Joseph François Dupleix (1697–1763), the French governor of Pondicherry, played what became known as the "Nabob Game" in southern India: buying the loyalty of local rulers and keeping them in line with *sepoys* (local troops) trained and armed by, and ultimately loyal to, France.

When France and Britain joined the War of the Austrian Succession, Dupleix raised the standard on behalf of French interests in India. In 1746 he captured Madras from the English, and in 1748 he withstood the British siege of Pondicherry. However, Dupleix failed to attract the governmental support he needed to take all of the south.

Dupleix's British rival was the natural adventurer Robert Clive (1725–1774). He built up a highly efficient army that fought with distinction against France. He went on to expel the Dutch and other foreign powers from India and to lay the foundations of the British Raj. In 1755 he was appointed lieutenant-governor of Fort St. David, near Madras; in the following year, Clive was sent to retake Calcutta after it was seized by the rebellious *nawab* of Bengal. He went further, inflicting a decisive defeat on the *nawab* at the Battle of Plassey (1757), which brought Bengal under British rule. Clive pioneered a system of "dual government" that gave the British financial and military control while leaving a puppet *nawab* responsible for everyday administration and the judiciary. Under Clive, the East India Company plundered the vast wealth of Bengal's princes, seizing treasuries and extracting enormous fees for its revenue collecting and military services.

Such large sums of cash brought a culture of bribery and corruption, and when Clive returned to England in 1767 he had to face a parliamentary inquiry into his own role. After six years he was cleared, but the inquiry ruined him, and he committed suicide shortly after it made its report.

British interests in India prospered under Warren Hastings (1732–1818), who rose through the ranks of the East India Company to become governor of Bengal in 1771. A keen reformer and a skilled diplomat, Hastings was sympathetic to Indian customs and spoke several local languages. In 1773 he became the first governor-general of India, appointed by the British government to

Emperor Aurangzeb hunts deer in a Mughal watercolor from Niglais, *c.* 1660. The ruthlessness with which he pursued his personal ambition would bring about the demise of the entire Mughal dynasty and clear the way for the Europeans.

manage their financial and territorial concerns.

Hastings set out both to consolidate British gains and to further territorial advances. He defended land and created a network of subsidiary alliances, under which Indian rulers paid the East India Company for providing British troops to protect their territory. Failure to pay up was met with brute force. But like Clive before him, Hastings suffered a spectacular fall from grace. When he returned to England, he faced impeachment on charges of extortion. After several years he was finally acquitted, but the proceedings left him a bankrupt and broken man.

Warren Hastings enjoys the fruits of his administrative success in this Mughal painting *c.* 1782. He was as aware of India's manifold riches as were the Aryan and Mughal leaders who ruled the country before him.

By now many prominent British politicians were appalled by the way the East India Company conducted its business. When Lord Cornwallis was made governor-general in 1786, he introduced long-overdue reforms, but while these may have satisfied politicians in England, they were not enough to stem the growing discontent among Hindus, Muslims and Sikhs in India. With much of their own produce undercut by cheap British imports, many Indians found themselves impoverished by the empire. But religious issues were to provide the focus for their discontent. Although the British helped to abolish such practices as *suttee* (widows burning on their husband's funeral pyres), the British Raj seemed to be becoming increasingly insensitive to local belief, denouncing Hinduism as mere idol-worship and championing Christianity. When the ban on missionary travel to India was lifted in 1813, few Indians converted.

Uprisings throughout the early nineteenth century culminated in the rebellion of 1857, and the spark was religious. When the Bengal Army's Third Cavalry Regiment was issued with new rifles, British colonels demonstrated how to bite the greased paper tips off the cartridges used in the new guns. The *sepoys*, Indian troops under British command, refused to follow suit believing the grease contained both cow and pig fat, an affront to Hindu and Muslim alike. The British took this as mutiny, the touch-paper of rebellion was lit, and garrisons and cities rose up across northern India. Although the unrest was quashed and the British government took control of the country from the East India Company to signal a new age of rule, the march to independence had gained a critical momentum.

In 1885 members of India's urban, educated Hindu elite gathered in Bombay to found the Indian National Congress. A few gifted people emerged as spokesmen for their generation, Surendranath Banerjee (1848–1925), Gopal Gokhale (1866–1915) and Bal Gangadhar Tilak (1856–1920) the most prominent among them. At first their demands were mild: they wanted more governmental accountability and equality of opportunity. They did not want the British out of India (they had, after all, prospered under British rule themselves). This view changed after World War I, when India's contribution of massive quantities of troops and raw materials was met with a renewing of wartime restrictions. Protests came to a terrible climax in the Punjab in 1919, when Gurkha troops opened fire on an unarmed and peaceful protest in Amritsar, killing 379 civilians and wounding more than a thousand.

The atmosphere of bitterness and mistrust led to increasingly loud calls for an end to British rule. The cause was soon taken up by a soft-spoken Gujarati barrister named Mohandas Karamchand Gandhi (1869–1948). He became politicized by his experience of racial discrimination in South Africa, and on returning to India he began a campaign of nonviolent confrontation and civil disobedience, known as *satyagraha*, or "clinging to truth," against British policy in 1920. He was repeatedly imprisoned, but often continued his protest from his cell by fasting. When Congress found itself unable to maintain its policy of disobedience, Gandhi carried on alone and secured what was perhaps his greatest victory. His twenty-five-day march against a British salt tax, in 1930, led to mass strikes as he and thousands of others collected salt from the Dandi shore.

The tide had turned against the British, who opened talks with Indian leaders to discuss the future of the subcontinent. The main aim of all parties concerned was to create a formula for independence that would protect the rights of the Hindu minority in Bengal and the Punjab and the Muslim minority elsewhere.

Independence came in August 1947, and with it came partition. The rise in nationalism had disguised the growing divisions between Hindus and Muslims, who felt threatened by the advent of majority Hindu rule. The All-India Muslim League, founded in 1906, was conspicuously separate from the Indian National Congress. Gandhi's overtly spiritual leadership of Indian opposition to British rule—he was brought up in the Jain tradition of nonviolence—alienated Muslims still further. Under Mohammed Ali Jinnah (1876–1948) they secured the recognition of the nation of Pakistan ("land of the pure").

When the British flag came down over India, more than 10 million people crossed the borders between India and Pakistan. Amid the chaos of this mass migration, fighting broke out that claimed some 250,000 lives. The following year, Gandhi was shot by a Hindu extremist who feared his leader was too pro-Muslim. But as Jinnah attempted to settle his fledgling state, India's first prime minister, Jawaharlal Nehru (1889–1964), set about consolidating the advances made by a country that now accommodated both established Western institutions and diverse ancient beliefs.

The Caste System

In the Vedic age four distinct social divisions were recognized: **brahmin** *(priests),* **kshatriya** *(warriors and kings),* **vaishya** *(traders and farmers), and* **shudra** *(artisans), distinctions that still underlie the Indian caste system.*

Hindus are born into a *jati* (caste) that has a certain rank in a hierarchy of purity. Lower castes are deemed capable of polluting higher ones, while higher castes transmit purity down to the lower. In order to avoid contamination, it is essential to marry within your own caste and take up an appropriate profession.

The creation of this system is described in the *Rig Veda*: "When the gods divided the Man . . . the *brahmin* was his mouth, the warrior was made from his arms, his thighs became the *vaishya*, from his feet the *shudra* was born."

Today caste is no longer a legal barrier to education or occupation, and the lower castes have benefited from positive discrimination (affirmative action). However, *jati* remains a powerful social factor, and the "caste vote" an emotional political issue.

Social class and professional opportunity are so closely linked that menial tasks, such as street sweeping, are still reserved for those at the very bottom of the caste system.

CITY OF VICTORY

The ancient city of Hampi, or Vijayanagara, "City of Victory," was the capital of south India's most successful Hindu dynasty, which flourished between the 14th and 16th centuries. At its height, this Hindu kingdom included almost the entire peninsula south of the Krishna River. Hampi was the dynasty's jewel, famed for its fabulous wealth throughout the world as merchants and travellers came from far away to trade and wonder at the sights. But in 1565 the city was sacked by Muslim forces and left to crumble. Now it stands as a testament to the terrible power of a rising dynasty, echoing with the distant voices of the past.

Above: The sacred center of Hampi lies in rocky terrain by the banks of the Tungabhadra River. The tall tower of the Virupaksha temple, with its shrine to Shiva, is the city's focal point. In this part of the city there were also temples to Krishna and Vishnu. The royal center, two kilometers to the south, contained most of the residential areas, as well as the ceremonial buildings and palaces of the court.

Right: One of the most extraordinary features of the sacred center is this 22-ft (6.7-meter) high statue of the man-lion Narasimha, the fourth incarnation of Vishnu. Seated like a *yogi* on an elaborate throne, the piece was sculpted from a single boulder of granite in 1528.

Left: The Lotus Mahal was built for the women of the court and mixes Hindu and Muslim architectural styles indicating that despite continual battles with Muslim armies, Hampi was a cosmopolitan city. The palace also recalls the form of the lotus-flower, the throne on which Lakshmi, goddess of wealth and good fortune, sits.

Below: The Vitthala temple is one of the greatest artistic achievements of the Vijayanagaran age. Built in the 16th century, it comprises a series of complex buildings set within a courtyard. This shrine in the form of a chariot with stone wheels is said to house Vishnu's mount Garuda, king of the birds.

Left: The Vijayanagara kings built many temples and in so doing developed a style that was to have a lasting influence on Indian religious construction. The tall pyramidal towers decorated with myriad figures from the Hindu pantheon, known as *gopuras*, are their main architectural legacy.

At Hampi, they crowned gateways, in this case to one of the city's many colonnaded streets. Now restored to its former glory, this particular *gopura* suggests something of the grandeur that greeted traders and travellers, when the city was a thriving commercial center in the 15th century.

TALES OF THE EPIC DIVINITIES

To the Western eye, the vast number of Hindu gods and goddesses can be bewildering. But beyond this variety lies unity—the unchanging, indestructible divine reality known as *brahman* that, according to Hindus, exists in all things. Everything in the universe, every creature and plant, is a manifestation of *brahman* and thus contains an element of the divine.

The many gods reflect different aspects of the divine unity. So the two most popular forms of Hindu worship, the modern cults of Vishnu and Shiva, are not exclusive. Although there is rivalry between their followers, expressed in a wealth of myths that show Vishnu's superiority to Shiva or vice versa, each set of devotees believes that the other group's god is also a manifestation of the divine.

An image of the underlying unity between Vishnu, Shiva and other gods arose in the fourth century CE in the *trimurti*, or triad. The three gods in the triad are Shiva, Vishnu and Brahma, the creator god considered the progenitor of all living things. They are

Above: **The Kedareswar temple at Bhubaneshwar, Orissa, was built between the 7th and 15th centuries. At one time there may have been 7,000 such shrines here.**

sometimes shown as three faces on a single statue symbolizing three distinct functions: Vishnu as the preserver of life, Brahma its creator and Shiva the destroyer of all things at the end of each cycle of time. Shiva and Vishnu are also worshipped in some parts of India as the single god Harihara (Hari being a title for Vishnu and Hara one of Shiva's many names).

The religious history of India is one of accumulation. Gods who declined in popularity were not discarded but modified. The gods' and goddesses' qualities, attributes, characteristics and roles are fluid over time. The cult of Shiva, for instance, has its origins in that of the Aryan storm god Rudra, in phallus cults and in the worship of the Lord of the Beasts, a fertility god venerated by the pre-Aryan Indian peoples. Throughout history, one god or spirit has been identified as an incarnation of another and so newer gods have been linked to older ones. Even mere mortals have benefited from this inclusive attitude, for the legendary Prince Rama was incorporated into divine mythology as an incarnation of Vishnu (see chapter 3).

Opposite: **This 18th-century painting shows women praying to Shiva's *lingam*, the life-giving phallus that confirmed Shiva as greatest of the gods. Within the temple stands the female *yoni*, a unifying counterbalance.**

27

Creation and Sacrifice

In Indian origin myths, the creator god does not, strictly speaking, create. Rather than make the universe out of nothing, he rearranges preexisting matter – often in an act of ritual sacrifice. Order emerges from chaos as the Earth is set apart from the waters and the sky.

Two hymns of the *Rig Veda* attribute the creation to a great being filled with wisdom and strength and with eyes, mouths, arms and feet on all sides. He is Visvakarman, the "Maker of All." His act of bringing things into order is a ritual sacrifice like that performed by priests, but he is also the sacrifice itself. The composers of the hymns make it clear that no one can really know the true nature of Visvakarman's sacrifice but the result, the separation

Two women on a terrace make ritual offerings to Brahma, in this watercolor from Khambavati Ragini, *c.* 1725. The importance that ritual came to assume in the Vedic age enhanced both the mystery of creation and the prestige of local priests.

of the Earth and sky, is clear enough for all to see. The hymns also liken the way in which Visvakarman produced order from chaos to a farmer churning milk to make butter.

Towards the end of the Vedic period, *c.* 1200–900 BCE, when the Vedic hymns, including the *Rig Veda,* were collected (see page 12), priests began to emphasize the power of ritual sacrifice. They claimed that their sacrifices were re-enactments of creation and that their rituals did more than simply propitiate the gods—they served to maintain the very order of the universe.

The image of sacrifice as creation is expressed elsewhere in the *Rig Veda* in the story of Purusha, the primordial man. He took the form of a man with 1,000 heads, 1,000 eyes and 1,000 feet. The gods and sages came from Purusha, and they took his vast body and pinned it down for a sacrifice. In their rituals, Vedic priests gathered around a sacrificial fire and made offerings of oil, grain and clarified butter. This practice is explained in the myth: the hymns say that when Purusha was sacrificed, the clarified butter thrown into the fire became the season of spring, the fuel that burned was summer and the act of offering, autumn. The result of the sacrifice was a great supply of clarified butter, which the gods formed into all the birds and animals that fill the Earth and all the forms of sacred verses known to priests.

Then Purusha was cut into many pieces, from which the entire universe was created: the sky came from his head, the Earth from his feet and the air from his navel. The moon issued from his soul and the sun from his eyes. From his mouth came Indra, king of the gods (see pages 36–39), and Agni, the god of sacrificial fire; his breath became Vayu, the god of wind.

Prajapati's Tears

One creation myth from the **Taittiriya Brahmana,** *c. 900–700* BCE, *tells how Prajapati willed the universe into being, producing smoke and fire, which condensed into a vast sea.*

Prajapati emerged, but as soon as he was conscious, the Lord of All Creatures wept, for he could see no purpose in his existence. As he cried, his falling tears became the Earth. The tears he wiped away became the air, and those he brushed upwards became the overarching sky. He wanted offspring and settled down to practice religious austerities. He gave birth to demons, then put aside his body, which became night. He created himself anew, made men and women and cast his body aside, which became the moon. He then assumed a new self, creating the seasons from his armpits and the dusk and dawn from his body. Finally he made the gods from his mouth, and when he put aside this next body, it became the day.

In some versions of the Prajapati creation myth, the Lord of All Creatures emerged not from a fiery miasma, but from a lotus bloom that had been floating on the primal waters.

The four classes of ancient India also came from Purusha: the *brahmin* or priests from his mouth; the *kshatriya* or noble warriors from his arms; the *vaishya* or traders and farmers from his thighs; and the *shudra* or servants from his feet.

The tale of Purusha was also applied to Brahma (see pages 30–33), who was then generally considered to be the source of the caste system. Visvakarman was later linked with Prajapati ("Lord of All Creatures"), who is also identified with Brahma and with Shiva (see pages 40–49) and with Tvastr, the gods' blacksmith.

In another version of the Purusha story, told in the *Satapatha Brahmana, c.* 800 BCE, the universe was the soul of Purusha, and he came into existence when he became conscious and said, "I am." Overcoming his initial fearfulness, he desired company and willed himself into two pieces, male and female. His two parts made love, and from their union humankind was born.

The female Purusha was overcome with shame because their love was incestuous. She fled from her father-husband, turning herself into a succession of beasts. But each time Purusha also changed, caught up with her, and made love to her again. In this way, the two of them made all the animals on earth. Purusha also created Agni (god of fire) from his mouth and hands. In the version of this myth in the *Brihandaranyaka Upanishad, c.* 700 BCE, Purusha is linked with Brahma.

The First of the Gods

Brahma is often cast as the first of the gods. A personification of *brahman*, he is the consciousness that existed before anything else and that, in the first act of creation, willed itself into being. Brahma's essential roles are as creator god and giver of boons, or favors, to petitioners who perform acts of austerity.

One of the vast array of Indian creation myths tells how, in the first days, Brahma emerged from a golden egg to begin creation. According to this tale, when the universal consciousness, *brahman*, felt the desire to create living creatures it willed first the waters into being and then a seed to float on them. The seed became a golden egg that shone with the brightness of the sun. It contained Brahma, also known as Narayana because he was born of the waters, or *naras*. For one year Brahma existed inside the egg until his meditative power split it open. Coming forth, Brahma made the sky and the Earth from the two halves of the egg, and then began creating the rest of the universe. This account is given in an early Hindu text, the *Laws of Manu*, written during the first and second centuries BCE. In this period, Brahma was understood as a personal form of *brahman*, the reality underlying and preceding the universe. According to some scholars, the idea of a personal creator god developed first in the popular imagination and was only later accepted by the priests as spiritual history.

Brahma was therefore seen as the essence of all things. The entire universe existed through him. He was believed to be present both at the creation and the destruction of the universe, which according to Hindu cosmology is destroyed and then recreated in a never-ending cycle.

In this conception, Brahma experiences time very differently from mortals. Each day, or *kalpa,* in his life is equivalent to 4.32 billion Earth years. At the end of each of his days, Brahma sleeps, and his night is exactly the same length as his day. When he goes to sleep, the universe dissolves into watery chaos; when he awakes, Brahma recreates the universe. All living creatures that have not found liber-ation from the eternal cycles of birth, death and rebirth are reborn in the new universe according to the *karma* they have accumulated over their previous existences.

Each *kalpa* is divided into 1,000 *mahayugas* ("great ages"), and each of these is split into four *yugas* ("ages"), with particular characteristics. The Kritayuga was a golden age, lasting 1,728,000 years. Humans were happy and virtuous and worshipped a white god. In the Tretayuga, which lasted 1,296,000 years, virtue fell away by one quarter; humans were dutiful but they were sometimes in conflict. They worshipped a red god. In the Dva-parayuga, lasting 864,000 years, virtue half disappeared; there were many quarrels and much dishonesty, but many people still did right; the god was yellow. The current age, the Kaliyuga, will last for 432,000 years. People are dishonest and wicked, they crowd into vast cities and live like beggars. Natural disasters are common and rulers are tyrannical; only one quarter of virtue remains; the god is black. At the end of this age, Vishnu will appear on Earth astride his white steed Kalki. Everything will be destroyed and the universe prepared for the new creation, which will begin at the start of the next cycle.

This cycle is embedded within a still larger one. After 360 *kalpas*, Brahma is said to have lived one year, and his life lasts for 100 of these years—a total of 155.5 trillion Earth years. At the end of that vast epoch, Brahma himself will join in the general dissolution, and after a further 100 divine years of chaos, a new cycle will be inaugurated by a new Brahma. At this point, Brahma as creator god will separate from *brahman* as divine reality, for while Brahma can die and be reborn in a new

Three of Brahma's four heads are visible in this 10th-century sandstone statue. Each face represents a different facet of the creator god. He once had a fifth head, so he could see his beloved consort Sarasvati wherever she went, but it was destroyed by Shiva after an argument.

form, *brahman* always exists. Hindus believe that there is no end or beginning to the cycle of time, which is likened to a wheel eternally spinning, with the unmoving axis at its center, representing the impersonal divine reality, or *brahman*.

There is great conflict between Brahma and Shiva, however. This reflects the competition between the worshippers of the two gods. As far as scholars can tell, there was never a cult of Brahma, although one may have existed and been lost to history. As Hinduism developed over the centuries, though, strong cults grew up around the gods Vishnu and Shiva, and Brahma's role diminished. He remained a creator deity, but he was no longer seen as the personal form of *brahman*, for this

honor passed to either Vishnu or Shiva. Moreover, many myths were reworked to highlight Brahma's inferiority to these other gods, some even suggesting that Brahma was created by one of them, and not from the divine waters from which sprang the beginnings of the universe.

One popular version of the creation story, told by Vaishnavites, followers of Vishnu, casts Brahma as the creative force of Vishnu. They identified Vishnu with *brahman*, asserting that he had

This Pahari school painting, *c.* 1760, shows Vishnu reclining on the snake of eternity with Brahma, cradled in a lotus flower, representing his creative energy. As Vishnu meditates with his consort Lakshmi, he orchestrates the birth of the world.

existed before anything else. Using his *maya*, or creative power, he created a vastness of primordial waters and then rested, lying on the 100-headed serpent Ananta-Shesha, who represented eternity. As Vishnu meditated, or in some accounts even as he slept, his creative energy came forth from his navel in the form of a delicate lotus blossom. It rose, wavering, up in the air, and in its petals was Brahma. By the power of Vishnu, Brahma brought forth order, and the universe was created. This creation takes place at the beginning of each cycle of time. In some versions, the serpent Ananta-Shesha represents the accumulated *karma* of the lives lived in the previous *kalpa*, which determines the form of the new creation.

The Superiority of Shiva

In an important myth told by Shaivites, followers of Shiva, Brahma and Vishnu are forced to recognize Shiva's great status and his superiority over them. One day Vishnu and Brahma were disputing which of them was the prime creator and thus the most worthy of reverence. Back and forth their arguments went, as each countered the other. But finally they were silenced when, suddenly, a vast, fiery pillar reared up before them on the all-encompassing primal waters.

Brahma and Vishnu were astonished by the pillar's vast size and the brilliance of its flames, and they agreed that they must find its source. Brahma transformed himself into a swan and flew upwards along the column for 1,000 years, while Vishnu became a boar and plunged into the waters, travelling down along the column for the same period. Neither found the end, and they returned, aching and speechless with weariness, to their starting point. Then Shiva appeared to them, from inside the pillar, and they realized that the awesome column was Shiva's *lingam*, or life-giving sacred phallus (see box, page 44).

From that day, Brahma and Vishnu accepted that Shiva was without equal among the gods. They had come from him, they saw, and must therefore pay him homage. In another version of

Cycles of Creation

Just as there are many versions of the creation, so there are varying descriptions of the Hindu cosmos. All, however, rest on the tension between eternity and rebirth.

The snakes on this 18th-century game board lead to hellish states, while ladders climb to moral ones. Celestial squares above complete the picture of the Hindu cosmos.

The Earth is composed of seven circular continents, the central one set in a salty sea from whose center rises Mount Meru. To its south lies Bharatavarsa, the old name for India. Below repose demons and snakes amid the seven vertical layers of hell, while above shine the seven layers of heaven, at the top of which is *brahman*, the abode of perfect souls. Before the souls that escape the torment of hell stretch two paths: for perfected souls lies the Way of the Gods, which follows the northern course of the sun to the eternal peace of *brahman*; the Way of our Fathers charts the southern course of the sun, eventually returning its souls to Earth, where they are reborn. Thus the cycles of creation and destruction, of birth, death and rebirth reflect the journey of both the soul and the universe itself.

33

Four-Headed God of Wisdom

Images of Brahma show him with red skin and white robes astride a goose or sitting on a lotus. He has four heads, indicating the four directions of the compass, and four arms, representing the four **Vedas** *or scriptures. Once, however, a burning desire led him to create a fifth head.*

As guardian of the *Vedas*, Brahma is the god of wisdom; he is also revered as the greatest of all sages. One of his names is "Grandfather," because of his status as creator and source of all. But there are several explanations as to why he has four heads. One story tells how Brahma created a female consort, Sarasvati, from his own great energy. Her beauty was so delicate that he felt a powerful longing for her although she was his own daughter. He turned his passionate gaze on her, but the goddess's natural modesty made her flee from him.

She skipped away to Brahma's left and then to his right, then ran lithely behind him, but each time the god grew a new head so that he could feast his eyes upon her. Unable to escape on Earth, she leaped into the sky, but Brahma sprouted a fifth head to follow her with his eyes. Then the god caught hold of his daughter and made love to her. She gave birth to the first people.

Brahma lost his fifth head in a quarrel with Shiva. One day Brahma was drunk and filled with illicit desire for his own daughter, Sandhya, who was married to Shiva. When he approached Sandhya, she understood his lecherous intent and fled in the fleet form of a deer, but Brahma transformed himself into a strong-legged stag and galloped after her. Shiva saw Brahma pursuing his wife across the inky blue sky, and he felt anger rage within himself. Roaring with divine wrath, he seized a bow and quiver and loosed an arrow that flew so fast and so accurately that it cut off the stag's head at a single strike. Then the animal turned back into Brahma, with four heads, and the god abandoned the unseemly chase, humbly paying his respects to Shiva.

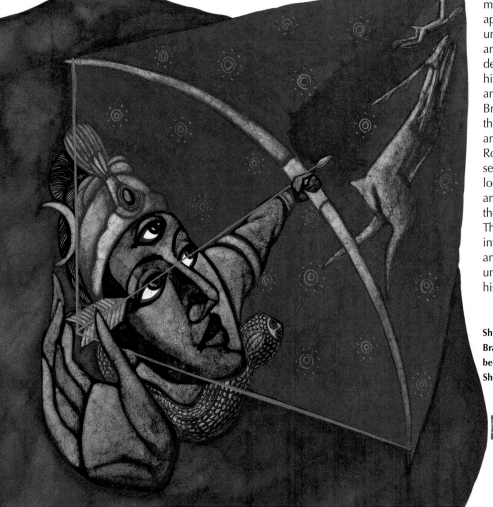

Shiva fires the deadly arrow that severs Brahma's fifth head. Shiva was angry because Brahma lusted after Sandhya, Shiva's wife.

Brahma, with his *shakti*, Sarasvati, rides the cosmic goose Hansa, which, like Shiva's bull and Vishnu's eagle, carries him throughout the world. Although the god eventually lost his status as the primary deity, this 1820s watercolor from Trichinopoly in southern India shows him in all his glory.

the myth, Brahma returned from his journey claiming that he had found the end of the *lingam*. But it soon became clear he was lying, and for this act of dishonesty he lost the right to be worshipped.

In later times Brahma's status diminished to such an extent that he came to feature in myths primarily as a granter of favors, or boons, to petitioners. Sometimes he was even forced to grant a boon because of the great spiritual power that the petitioner had gained through meditation or the performance of austerities—acts of physical self-denial and mental concentration. For example, in the tale of the Triple City of the demons (see pages 48–49) when the demons ask Brahma for permission to build their cities and to be made invincible for a limited period, he has to allow it, even though it is against the gods' interests, because of the power

they have gained by performing strict austerities. He also makes the demon Taraka invincible in combat with all the gods except a future son of Shiva (see pages 46–47) because of the demon's religious performance.

The petitioners are filled with *tapas* ("heat") and so cannot be denied. The power of *tapas* is derived from meditation and austerities. It is so strong that demons and even ordinary humans who possess it can overpower the gods. Throughout the *Mahabharata* (see pages 78–89), men and demons cause trouble for the gods. This is an unfamiliar concept for Western readers accustomed to the mythological world of the Greeks and Romans in which gods occasionally descend to help or punish humans but in which humans seldom, if ever, affect the lives of gods.

35

The Bringer of Plenty

The hymns of the *Rig Veda* praise Indra again and again for his power and virile strength. Quick to act, he had a vast golden body, great arms bursting with muscles and a distended belly swollen from his delight in the gods' intoxicating drink of *soma*.

Indra's role as storm god, master of the rainclouds, won him the adulation of a people saved from drought and famine by the welcome onslaught of the monsoon rains. A divine warrior, a storm divinity armed with thunderbolts, as well as a god of fertility and the life-giving waters, he occupied the supreme position among the gods of the Vedic age. His status later diminished, but he remained an important Hindu god and, as Shakra, became a significant Buddhist deity (see page 119).

According to the *Rig Veda* myths, within moments of his birth Indra, the great ruddy-faced warrior, took up the powerful *vajra* ("thunderbolt") and, afire with the force of the divine drink *soma* (see box opposite), sprang into action to defend men from drought. The demon Vritra had rounded up the raincloud cattle and imprisoned them in his ninety-nine fortresses. Drought had already taken a deadly grip on the Earth, bringing men and women closer to starvation each day. Ceaselessly they appealed to the gods for help.

The divine response was quick to come. Indra was born, son of Dyaus (sky) and Prithivi (Earth). The infant at once grabbed the *soma* that men were offering to the gods and drank a vast amount of it. He was filled with divine power, and in that instant, he became lord of the three worlds of the Earth, the sky and the air between.

He seized the thunderbolt that belonged to his father Dyaus and leaped into a golden chariot. At his side were the Maruts, spirits of tempest and thunder, who were to become Indra's stalwart fol-

A wall-painting of Indra from Balawaste, *c.* 7th–8th century CE. The great storm god may have declined in importance since the Vedic age, but his influence is still felt among the newer deities.

lowers. The Maruts took the form of fearless youths in golden armor equipped with axes, bows and arrows and dazzling lightning spears. In chariots drawn by deer, they rode out with Indra against Vritra and, like a shower of rain that comes with the onrush of a violent storm, they scattered forth across the sky, chanting songs of war.

Vritra watched Indra approach and roared as the young god drew near. The demon was complacent because he thought no god or man could hurt him. But Indra, fired by the divine drink, proved deadly with his fearsome thunderbolt, finding the monster's weak spots and quickly dispatching him. On galloped the Maruts and set the cloud cattle free in a great stampede, so that the waters gushed down from the sky to the Earth below. As the thunder rumbled, lightning flashed and the storms broke, men and women danced for joy on the parched ground and hailed Indra, who had saved them from the drought.

Vibrant with triumph, Indra then turned against his father Dyaus. Taking him by the ankle, he flung Dyaus to the ground and killed him, ignoring his mother Prithivi's pleas to spare her husband. Taking his father's fearsome thunderbolt as his own, Indra, although still only newborn, proved his status as one of the great gods.

Dyaus was often associated with Varuna ("All-Encompassing"), another god of the Vedic era, and

Drink of the Gods

Indra's heroic exploits were fuelled by the divine intoxicant soma, a strong milky liquor that was a key part of religious sacrifices in the Vedic period.

The vital life-sustaining liquid, the drink of the gods also known as *amrita* (see box, page 38), was believed to make all who tasted it immortal.

In time, the sacred liquid was personified as the god Soma. Like Indra, he was a warrior and because Indra relied on the drink for his strength, Soma was sometimes said to rank higher among the deities than the storm god himself. Soma assumed Indra's role as god of waters and fertility and became associated with the moon and the moon god Chandra. In some myths, the *soma* of the gods was kept in the moon, which waned and waxed as it was drunk or refilled.

Soma may have derived from a hallucinogenic mushroom, fly agaric. It is not found in India, but the Aryans may have known it because it does grow in Afghanistan and Europe.

The eagle Garuda, shown here in a teak carving dating from the 17th century, incurred Indra's wrath when he stole the divine *amrita*.

The Churning of the Milk

The great powers of Indra were waning because he had been cursed by a powerful sage. The gods were worried that if their leader grew weak, they would be overcome by their enemies, the demons. So Vishnu instructed them to churn the Ocean of Milk to create the divine drink soma, *or* amrita.

goddess Lakshmi, who became Vishnu's wife, appeared. Next came Vishnu's white steed and the white elephant Airavata, which Indra claimed. A flood of blue poison rose up, but before it could devastate the Earth, Shiva gulped it down, keeping it in his throat, which is why he is called Nilakantha ("Blue Throated"). Finally, the divine physician Dhanwantari rose up from the ocean, holding a cup full to the brim with *soma*.

The cunning demons turned against the gods and stole the *soma*. Vishnu, dressed as a seductive woman, managed to return it to the gods, but the demon Rahu, disguised as a god, at last got a taste. The sun and moon warned Vishnu, and although Rahu was killed, the demon's head and neck were infused with the *soma*, rendering him immortal. He flew up into the sky and to this day wages war on the sun and moon, and sometimes even swallows them, causing an eclipse.

Then the demons and gods fought a tremendous, pitched battle. Thousands upon thousands fell as the gods triumphed. They returned Mount Mandara to its proper place, and trooped home, rejoicing loudly. The wondrous Vishnu became guardian of the *soma*.

So great was the undertaking that Vishnu ordered both gods and demons to bring the great Mount Mandara to the ocean's edge to stir the waters with. They balanced it on the back of the king of tortoises, Kurma, one of Vishnu's many incarnations (see pages 57–61), and used the great serpent Vasuki, or Ananta, as a churning rope to twist the mountain and so stir up the waters. They soon tired, but lightning burst from Vasuki's mouth and unleashed a welcome, cooling rainstorm. Trees on Mount Mandara were torn from their roots by the

This Pahari school watercolor, *c.* 1760, shows Vishnu and the serpent, Vasuki, churning the milky ocean to produce the divine drink *soma*.

motion and, rubbing against each other, burst into flames. Soon the entire mountain was ablaze, and all the animals and plants that lived on it were destroyed. When Indra put the fire out with rain, juices from the trees and plants flowed into the ocean and over the gods, making them immortal.

As the gods and demons churned, the moon arose, followed by the sun; then the

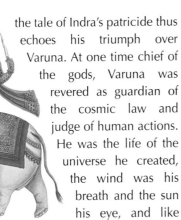

the tale of Indra's patricide thus echoes his triumph over Varuna. At one time chief of the gods, Varuna was revered as guardian of the cosmic law and judge of human actions. He was the life of the universe he created, the wind was his breath and the sun his eye, and like Indra after him, he was the giver of waters. Varuna punished mortals for their wrongdoing, and images of the god show him carrying a rope with which to tie up sinners. But in the course of the Vedic age, Varuna's authority diminished, and he lost his pre-eminent position. In later times, Varuna became a god of rivers and seas.

Indra's conflict with Varuna is a reflection of the clash in the Vedic age between the *brahmins* (priests), whose loyalty was to Varuna, and the *kshatriyas* (warrior class), whose special god was Indra. The active Indra seized the initiative, representing the power of the warriors' actions, as opposed to the cosmic law embodied by Varuna. Indra's thundering progress across the heavens with the warlike Maruts make him symbolic of the raiding warriors of the Vedic age. In the tale of Vritra, he and the Maruts round up the cloud cattle just as bands of warlike Aryans would have raided the cattle of other tribes.

Indra assumed many of the characteristics of Varuna, and he was even praised as the creator of the universe in one of the *Rig Veda* hymns. According to this account, he built it in the form of a simple wooden house: first he took the measure of space and the sun, then he built four corner posts on which he hung the walls of the universe; and finally he set the sky on top as the roof. Two of the doors of the universe-house opened to the east, and each morning Indra flung them wide to let the sun in. At the end of the day, Indra took the sun and hurled it out of the world's west-facing doors, into the surrounding darkness.

The Guardian of Fertility

As source of the life-giving waters, Indra was also revered as a fertility god. One story tells how the demons, seeing that the gods were sustained by the ritual sacrifices of priests, defiled the plants that the priests used so that their sacrifices would be spoiled. The plants withered, and all the fruits turned to foul-tasting mush; men and their animals grew idle and listless, and famine descended on the land. Then the gods struck back, making their own purifying sacrifices that banished the poison and restored the fertility of the Earth. Men and animals could eat once more and make offerings to the gods. Happiness at last returned to the Earth, and a great festival of thanksgiving was planned to celebrate the famous victory.

But among the gods, there was a disagreement as to who should be first to accept the offerings of the grateful people. The deities arranged a race and declared that the winner should assume the honor. The victors were Indra and his brother Agni, the fire god, and it was they who were duly honored. Ever afterwards, Indra was celebrated as a fertility god. Offerings of the new crop were made to the two sibling deities each and every year at the autumn rice harvest and the spring barley harvest.

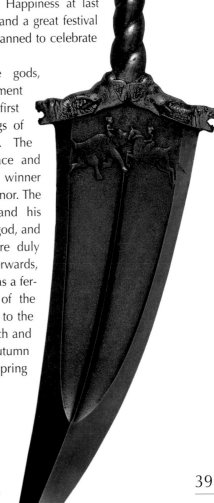

This 17th-century dagger is decorated with elephants, animals associated with Indra (above) in his manifestation as god of war.

39

God of Destruction, Lord of Life

With Brahma the creator and Vishnu the preserver, the third god of the Hindu *trimurti* or triad is Shiva, whose primary aspect is as the destroyer. But he is an enigmatic god with many attributes that frequently seem contradictory.

Shiva is both mountain mystic and erotic dancer, kindly protector and fierce destroyer. He is worshipped in the form of the *lingam*, or phallus, but also possesses female energy and is sometimes seen as the androgynous god-goddess Ardhanarishvara.

He has five principal aspects, each with many forms. The first is an ash-smeared ascetic, who sits in his heaven on Mount Kailasa, in the Himalayas. His devotions are the source of all his power and maintain the entire universe.

The second is Nataraja, Lord of the Dance, who embodies and celebrates the movement of the universe and rhythm of life. His is both a dance of joy—his footsteps relieve the suffering of his worshippers—and the *tandava*, the dance of destruction that returns all to chaos at the end of each *kalpa* (see page 30). Sometimes the dance is said to represent the rhythm of the individual's consciousness in which illusion and knowledge are in perpetual conflict.

The third aspect is a fearsome destroyer. As Bhutesvara, Lord of Ghosts, Shiva is said to loiter in cremation grounds bedecked in terrifying snakes and hideous human skulls. Animal sacrifices are made to appease him. (In this aspect, he also has the form of Bhairava, demon-destroyer.)

In his fourth aspect, he is a fertility god. Common images of fertility such as snakes, bulls, *soma* and the crescent moon are associated with

The symbol Om (top left) denotes Shiva, whose meditations on Mount Kailasa nourished the universe. This 18th-century painting, above, shows him attended by Parvati and devotees.

him. He is attended by a bull, Nandi, and has an image of the crescent moon on his forehead.

The fifth and final aspect is a benign protector, god of medicine, healer and giver of long life. He uses his hair to prevent the force of the Ganges River creating devastation on the Earth as it tumbles down from heaven (see pages 50–51). He is the loving consort of the goddess Parvati and together they symbolize wholeness. When he is worshipped as the phallic *lingam* (see pages 44–45), it is in conjunction with the encircling *yoni* (which represents both the vagina and the womb). The union of *yoni* and *lingam* represents the harmony between matter and spirit as well as of male and female. By uniting with his *shakti*, or female energy, sexual difference is resolved into wholeness.

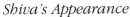

Shiva's Appearance

This god is sometimes represented as a fair-skinned man, with five faces smeared with ashes. These stand for the five directions – north, south, east, west and the zenith – for Shiva's power is all-encompassing. His many hands represent balance, between life and death, good and evil. His hair is usually in long, matted locks, sometimes curled on top, and he often wears snakes around his neck, with one curled in his hair. His throat is blue because as the protector, he swallowed the blue poison that was produced when the Ocean of Milk was churned. Shiva carries the *trisula*, or trident, representing lightning, a sword and a bow, which he used to destroy the dreaded Triple City (see pages 48–49), and a club with a skull at the end.

He has a third eye in his forehead that appeared one day when Parvati came up behind him and in loving jest covered his two eyes. But when Shiva could not see, darkness flooded through the universe, and the third eye appeared to ward off chaos, sending flames into the dark. It burned Parvati's father Himalaya and all the creatures in the universe. But Parvati begged Shiva for mercy, and he brought Himalaya and the creatures back to life. He also used his third, fiery eye to kill the god of love, Kama (see page 47).

Shiva and Rudra

Shiva's terrible aspects are derived from his links to Rudra, fearsome Vedic god of cattle, storms and medicine.

The name Shiva ("Auspicious One") was used as a title for Rudra until the end of the Vedic era. Rudra ("Howler"), with both destructive and life-giving aspects, was seen as a wild man riding a bull. He was also god of sacrifices and song, the gods' physician and guardian of healing herbs. In addition, he was identified with Agni, god of sacrificial fire, and offered protection against Varuna, the mysterious judge of men (see page 39). Shiva inherited these characteristics from Rudra, but also had links to pre-Aryan deities such as the god of Yoga, worshipped by the peoples of the Indus Valley. Another influence was the Lord of the Beasts, to whom animal sacrifices were made. This god contributed to Shiva's aspect as both fearsome destroyer of the universe and benign fertility god.

Agni, the Vedic god of fire, adorns the Brahmesvara temple, Bhubaneshwar. Unlike Rudra, he lost neither his name nor his status when he was absorbed into the Hindu pantheon.

41

Lord of the Dance

In his aspect as Nataraja, Lord of the Dance, Shiva contains and expresses the movement and energy of the universe and of life itself. The rhythm of the dance is sometimes gentle and soothing, sometimes fervent and terrible.

Shiva is at once the great ascetic, pictured above, and the energetic Lord of the Dance *(right)*. The painting is from Bilsamer, Rajasthan, while the bronze statue is from southern India and dates from the 19th–20th century.

Nataraja's dance is the movement of creation and also the *tandava*, dance of destruction, that plunges the universe back into primordial chaos at the end of each *kalpa* (see pages 30–33). It is the rhythm arising from the creative conflict of opposites—knowledge and illusion, good and evil, destruction and creation—that is embodied by Shiva. It stands for cosmic truth. In his aspect as protector, Shiva uses the dance to relieve the sufferings of his worshippers. The dance also expresses Shiva's glory as a god, and all who see it are filled with awe. The gods themselves are said to gather to watch and, if Shiva dances in a cremation ground, he tames even the demons.

Symbolism of the Dancing Figure

Images of Shiva as Nataraja began to appear around the medieval period. They represent Shiva's attributes and aspects of his godhead. Nataraja's many hands stand for the opposites he encompasses. He is shown dancing on the dead body of a demon, symbolizing ignorance and forgetfulness. He often holds a drum, representing creation, in one of his hands, while a flame standing for destruction sprouts from the palm of another. His raised leg signifies liberation, a spiritual release as flames arch around him. Shiva is worshipped in this form mainly in southern India.

One of the most celebrated of Shiva's myths tells how the god, unrecognized, danced for a group of ascetics in a Himalayan pine forest where the sages had settled to practice demanding religious austerities. (One of Shiva's own aspects was as an ascetic, who sat in deep meditation on top of Mount Kailasa in the Himalayas.) The myth explains the worship of Shiva in the form of the *lingam* or phallus (see box, page 44).

High in the mountain forest, where the green light flickered gently over bright banks of flowers and the birds sang sweetly, the sages were practicing many advanced forms of self-denial. Some ate nothing but green moss gathered from the dank and dripping caves, while others stretched out in icy mountain pools or wandered the landscape beneath great banks of clouds, refusing all shelter; they either sat meditating in the usual cross-legged yogic position, or stood, as if suspended, on the tip of a single toe.

One day a stranger arrived at the mountain retreat, where the sages lived with their wives and daughters. The man was naked, his pale skin smeared with grey ashes, his hair matted and untied. His wild appearance was matched by his

The Cult of the *Lingam*

Worship of the lingam, or phallus, is a central part of the cult of Shiva but dates from the time of the Indus Valley civilization.

One of Shiva's several aspects is as a god of fertility, and in his early form as Rudra (see box, page 41), he was closely linked to the ancient Lord of the Beasts who was worshipped in the Indus Valley around 2000 BCE, before the coming of the Aryans. Some evidence suggests that people of that era worshipped the phallus, or male sexual organ, and in time the practice attached itself to Shiva. The appearance of *lingam* worship in Hinduism itself can be dated to around 200 BCE when the first images and stone representations of *lingams* began to appear.

This red sandstone *lingam* is from central India, c. 15th century. Phallus worship has its roots in one of the oldest cults of Indian religious history.

Lingams and *yoni* are used as images of the unity lying beneath the various manifestations of the universe – the single indestructible divine reality, or *brahman*. This is also represented by Shiva and his goddess Shakti, or by Shiva's androgynous form as Ardhanarishvara, who is half-man, half-woman.

The first *lingams* were symbolic representations of the penis, but in later times the image became more highly stylized and often had a face of Shiva carved upon it. There are many myths explaining the origin of *lingam* worship (see pages 40–43) in which the god's *lingam* is cut off by himself or others and then worshipped as an image of Shiva's power and all-pervasiveness.

---

unpredictable behavior—he sang with a wide smile, then danced intensely in a frenzy of sexual energy; at other times he cackled with laughter and screamed wildly. The sages' wives were aroused by the stranger's erotic dance, and they gathered close around him as he came up to the retreat house, lasciviously watching his naked gyrations.

Enraged, the sages came running to confront him. They spat curses at him, calling him a demon. But all the religious power and energy they had nurtured had no effect on the stranger because he was the great god Shiva in disguise.

The priests still did not recognize his divinity. They upbraided him for his behavior, for it was not seemly, they said, for an ascetic to behave in such a manner. He should put on a loincloth and either cover up his *lingam* or cut it off if he wanted to be worthy of respect.

Shiva still kept his identity a secret. In the form of this ragged man, he spoke kindly to the sages. He told them that no god or man, however spiritually powerful, could force him to cast aside his *lingam*, but that he was willing to use his own power to remove it. The sages were pleased with this reply, and they invited the man to stay in the retreat. At this Shiva glowed with delight. Still in disguise, he cut off the great *lingam* and then faded into the mountain air.

But Shiva's action had terrible consequences. When he cast aside the *lingam*, order collapsed in the universe. The sun's power failed and sacrificial rituals lost their effectiveness. The seasons fell out of their appointed order, and the constellations of the night sky wandered aimlessly, far from their ordained paths. The sages' own vitality faded, and though they held fast to their familiar religious practices, they even began to lose their sure faith in the rightness of *dharma*, the universal order.

Then the sages went to Brahma for help. They prostrated themselves before the god and told him of the strange, ash-daubed ascetic. They told Brahma that the stranger had seduced their wives and daughters and that they had persuaded him to cut off his *lingam*. They had caused a crisis in the world below, they said, and they begged Brahma to tell them how to put matters right.

Brahma listened and meditated deeply on the problem. When he was ready to speak, he told the sages that the ascetic who had visited them was none other than the lord Shiva. The way to win Shiva's favor, Brahma said, was to make an image of the *lingam* for use in their worship. Shiva would then visit them once more, and when they saw him, they would be cleansed of their ignorance and *adharma,* lawlessness.

The sages paid homage to Brahma and went back to the pine forest, where they did as he had instructed them. Brahma's words

proved right—the seasons moved once again into their rightful path and the sages' own virility returned. For a full year, they worshipped Shiva, using images of the *lingam*.

When spring came, Shiva returned. The sages gathered round in worship and asked his forgiveness. Shiva spoke gently to them, saying that they would be cleansed by the ashes of sacrificial fires because they contained his own seed; these ashes alone could bring worshippers into contact with the god they sought. With great joy, the sages took their images of the *lingam* and washed them in fragrant waters mixed with flowers. Then they washed the great god himself, singing gently.

A granite form of Nandi, Shiva's principal means of travel, from Rajasthan, *c.* 16th–17th century. Embodying sexual energy, the bull was once the ancient Vedic Lord of Joy, Nandikeshvara.

The Battles Between Fertility and Love

As the deity in which opposites are reconciled, Shiva was both a great yogic ascetic and a procreative fertility god. As a sage dedicated to practicing austerities, he was an enemy of Kama, the god of love; as fertility god, brimful of virility, he was in competition with him. So it was not long before this unremitting rivalry erupted into violent conflict.

A demon, Taraka, performed a series of such powerful austerities that Brahma was compelled to grant him anything he wished as a boon. The demon asked Brahma to make him invulnerable to any of the gods—and to grant that he could only be killed by a future son of Shiva. Brahma had no choice but to grant the wish. Then Taraka, glorying in his invulnerability, attacked the gods and swept all before him, taking their wives hostage. Vishnu, armed with his fearsome discus, challenged Taraka, and they fought night and day for 30,000 years without stopping once. But Taraka could not be harmed, and Vishnu finally abandoned the fight and fled. Seeing this and despairing now of recovering their wives, the gods travelled to Brahma to ask for help.

Brahma told the gods of the boon he had been forced to grant the demon. Since Taraka was vulnerable only to Shiva's offspring, the only hope of ending the demon's reign of terror lay in persuading Shiva to pause from his religious austerities in order to make love with his goddess-consort Parvati and thus provide an heir who would be able to deal with Taraka as they wished. The gods travelled to the very top of Mount Meru, where

Shiva was said to meditate within mountains such as the Lapchi Kang peaks, in Helambu, Nepal.

Vishnu had taken refuge, shaking with fear at the thought of the demon Taraka. Vishnu was comforted that a solution had been found.

Then Indra set his mind to the problem, and he thought of the god of love, Kama. Indra knew that Kama boasted of being all-powerful. The love god carried a bow and a quiver of five arrows, one made from the sun lotus, one from a flower named the asoka, one from mango, one from jasmine and the fifth from the blue lotus. When these weapons hit home, they could provoke in their victim each stage of love—infatuated interest, excitement, wilting, warming and stiffening. Kama was aware that Indra had thought of him, and he flew to see what he wanted. Indra explained that the gods needed Kama to disrupt Shiva's awesome concentration and awake in him desire for Parvati.

Kama took his weapons and flew to Mount Kailasa, where he met Nandi, Shiva's attendant, who had taken a form almost identical to Shiva himself, with four arms and three eyes. Tall as a mountain, Nandi blocked the way, but the ever-resourceful Kama transformed himself into a soft, sweet-smelling breeze from the south. Nandi sighed and smiled gently as Kama wafted past him.

The love god was filled with joy when he saw blue-necked Shiva, shining like a gem or a pure sacrificial fire, meditating deeply with all his energy. Kama drew his all-powerful bow, preparing to loose one of his arrows, then paused, frozen in the same pose for 60 million years, until Shiva stirred and opened two of his three eyes.

Shiva's gaze fell on Parvati, who was also practicing austerities close by. The sight pleased him, but he felt suspicious and thought that Kama, the mischievous love god, must be near at hand. Shiva looked across the mountainside, and when he saw Kama, a blast of flame emerged from his third eye, consuming the love god in an instant.

Shiva looked kindly on Parvati and asked her if she desired anything. She replied that with the god of love dead, there was nothing Shiva could give her. At this, Shiva insisted that he had not meant to kill Kama; he said that the power of his third eye had dispatched the intruder by itself.

A princess lies powerless before Kama's arrows of love in this Pahari school miniature, c. 1790. Shiva did not prove quite so yielding and, despite being made to fall for Parvati, destroyed Kama for his insolent challenge to his own authority.

Again he asked Parvati if she wished for a boon, for she had earned the right by her faithfulness. This time the goddess asked Shiva to restore Kama to life so he could bring warmth to the world. To please the goddess, Shiva decreed that Kama should rise from death, but without a body since this had been turned to ashes. Kama rose up and went out into the world, travelling where he pleased with his bow and five arrows. Shiva made love to Parvati, and she gave birth to Skanda, who was also known as Karttikeya—and when he grew up, he killed the demon Taraka.

47

The Destruction of the Triple City

Shiva's role as destroyer inspired the tale of his attack on the Triple City of the demons. The three cities represented the three worlds of Earth, air and sky, and Shiva's annihilation of them reflects his destruction of the universe at the end of each *kalpa* (4.32 billion years).

In the days shortly after the great battle in which the gods defeated the demons and Shiva's son Skanda dispatched the mischievous Taraka, Taraka's three sons Tarakaksa, Kamalaksa, and Vidyunmalin took themselves to a mountain top and built up a great store of *tapas*-power by practicing meditation and austerities. Then they visited Brahma to ask for a boon, and because of their strict observances, he agreed to their wish.

Their first request was to be made immortal. As this went entirely against *dharma*, the universal law, Brahma was able to turn it down. Then the demons asked for three cities in which they could live for 1,000 years, until Shiva came to destroy them at the appointed time.

The sole surviving seaside temple at Mahabalipuram on the Coromandel coast has two shrines, the larger one on the right celebrating Shiva, the one on the left Vishnu. Built by Rajasimha, 700–728 CE, there were originally seven temples in the area.

Brahma granted their wish and the three sons of Taraka asked the demon Maya to construct their three cities. The first, of gold, he built in heaven; it was ruled by Tarakaksa. The second, made of silver, hung in the air; its king was Kamalaksa. The third, of iron, stood on the Earth and was subject to Vidyunmalin. All three were wondrous to behold, and the three demon kings ruled them for many years. As their reputation grew, millions upon millions of demons came to live with them.

At this time King Tarakaksa's son, Hari, won Brahma's good will by undergoing a strict program of self-denial and meditation. As a boon, Hari asked for a lake with the power of restoring life to demon warriors who had died. With the powers that Brahma granted, the demons ravaged the Earth. Because they did not fear death, they were unstoppable in battle, and they soon began greedily taking possession of the entire celestial realm.

Even fearsome Indra, attacking the demon cities with the Maruts, could not break down their defenses. The gods, despairing, trudged off to ask Brahma for help. He listened kindly to their complaints and said that because the demons had gone against *dharma*, they could be destroyed, but he added that only one weapon, a single arrow fired by Shiva, could bring the Triple City low.

The gods at last persuaded Shiva to fight for them. He asked for a chariot, bow and arrow with which to do battle. Shiva then leapt into the chariot and, with Brahma at the reins, set off for the Triple City. When he was within sight of the demons, Shiva loosed an arrow, and the demons and their city were consumed in a wall of fire. Shiva paused and told the flames to cease because it was not yet time for the end of the universe. But all the gods, people and creatures gave thanks to Shiva, who had saved them from the demons.

Tvastr, the Divine Artisan

The divine artisan Tvastr, creator of Shiva's chariot, made weapons for the gods, including Indra's fearsome thunderbolt. He was also the architect of celestial palaces.

For Varuna, god of waters, Tvastr (also known as Visvakarman) fashioned a dwelling place that floated like an island far out to sea. He raised a white-walled hall and surrounded it with trees made of precious jewels. Here Varuna held court, adorned with flowers and attended by the Adityas, sons of the goddess Aditi, who were a source of prosperity. Varuna's other servants were *nagas*, hooded snakes, and a host of giants and demons who won release from death and rebirth by making vows of loyalty. In the many rooms and spacious seats of the great hall lived the spirits of seas, rivers and mountains. Day after day the halls resounded with dancing and hymns in praise of Varuna.

For the storm god Indra, Tvastr built a heaven named Swarga, fashioned like a chariot, and for Yama, god of the dead (see box, page 89), an assembly house the color of glittering gold, filled with sweet smells and gentle melodies.

Holy Waters, Blessed Earth

Hindus believe that the Ganges is a holy river that can purify those who bathe in it. One myth relates that the Ganges flowed only in heaven until Shiva helped it run upon the Earth, releasing thousands of souls who had been punished by the gods.

On Earth, Sagara, King of Ayodha, was desperate for his two wives to conceive because he felt incomplete without offspring. He performed rites of abstinence and other austerities, after which his first wife produced one son but his second wife, Sumati, gave birth to 60,000. These were called the Sagaras. But they grew up to be such unruly children that the gods complained to Vishnu, who decided to punish them.

One day, Sagara chose his finest stallion to make an *ashvamedha*, or ritual horse sacrifice, as an expression of his great power and wide dominion. For a whole year he wandered the Earth with his horse, challenging all he encountered. He even wished to fight Indra, but the great god, angry at such pride, seized the horse, and drove it to the realm of Patala, far beneath the Earth.

The proud king ordered the 60,000 Sagaras to dig towards the center of the Earth in the hope of discovering Patala. Eventually they came to a place far underground where the horse was grazing, guarded by Kapila, a sage who was a partial incarnation of Vishnu. The Sagaras mistook him for Indra and began insulting him. But they angered Kapila too much, and in revenge he reduced all 60,000 young men to a pile of ashes.

Sagara was distraught and sent his grandson Ansuman to beg Kapila for mercy. The sage relented and said that the Sagaras would be raised from death on the day the sacred Ganges left heaven and descended to water the Earth. Many years later, Ansuman's grandson Bhagiratha Raja

The sacred Ganges streams through Shiva's hair and out into the fields. This picture from the Punjab Hills in Rajasthan, c. 1730, reflects the belief that while the river's source is Vishnu's toe, it is through Shiva that the waters flow from heaven to Earth.

The Sacred Ganges

The Ganges rises in the Himalayas and flows for more than 1,550 miles (2,500 kilometers) to the Bay of Bengal. It is the holiest of the three rivers of Hinduism.

According to myth, the Ganges flows from Vishnu's toe through heaven, Earth and the underworld. The three streams meet at Benares, or Varanasi, the most sacred city in India, also called Kashi ("City of Light") and said to be the home of Shiva himself.

The beautiful goddess Ganga, personification of the river, was said to be a daughter of Himalaya, god of the mountain range. She was first a consort of Vishnu, but he considered one wife to be enough and passed her on to Shiva. She also married a mortal king, Shantanu. The eight *vasus*, gods of day, wind, fire, water, dawn, light, moon and the Pole Star, had been cursed to be born as mortals; Ganga promised to be their mother and to kill them as soon as they were born so they could return to immortal life. She kept her promise for the first seven *vasus* but then her Earthly husband stopped her hand. The eighth survived to become Bhishma, one of the heroes of the *Mahabharata*.

The peaks of Bhagirathi Parbat tower over the Ganges headwaters in the Indian Himalayas.

won a boon from Brahma and Shiva, so he asked the gods to allow the Ganges to flow on Earth. The great gods agreed, but they saw that the force of the celestial river might cause devastation on Earth if it was not dissipated in some way. Shiva then offered to check the power of the river by letting it flow through his matted hair. This divided the waters into seven rivers—the Ganges itself and its tributaries. The life-giving waters ran quickly across the grateful Earth, but did not flood it. They filled the deep hole left by the 60,000 Sagaras, creating the ocean (also called *sagara*). The waters cascaded into the underworld, where they covered the ashes of the 60,000 Sagaras. In that instant, the young men's souls rose to the heavens.

THE WATERS OF PURIFICATION

There are three holy rivers in India – the Yamuna, the old Sarasvati and, greatest of all, the Ganges. This mighty stream flows through the very heart of the country, providing a focus for nearly half of India's population. For centuries, the Gangetic plains have been a major source of food and textile production, coveted by successive waves of invaders. But it is as a spiritual symbol that the river is most potent. And of the pilgrimage sites that lie along its course, none is as sacred as the city of Varanasi.

The Ganges' 1553-mile (2500-kilometer) journey from the Himalayas to the Bay of Bengal is punctuated by holy sites that attract millions of pilgrims a year.

The temple at Gangotri (which means "source of the Ganga") is the closest to its source. At 10,302 feet (3140 meters), it stands above the pilgrimage town of Rishikesh, which watches over the river as it heads towards Hardwar, one of India's seven sacred cities (the others are Mathura, Ujjain, Dwaraka, Ayodhya, Kanchipuram and, most holy of all, Varanasi). Pilgrims come here to bathe in and collect the pure waters and, every twelve years, to celebrate the great festival of Kumbha Mela.

Allahabad is the next main pilgrimage destination, a city that marks the Ganges' sacred confluence with the Yamuna River and the now-dry Sarasvati. It is also said that the god Brahma himself once offered a sacrifice here.

At the mouth of the Ganges lies Sarga Island, revered as the home of Sagara, father of the 60,000 Sagaras—the unruly children turned to ashes by Vishnu. Sagara was also the great-great grandfather of Bhagiratha Raja, who brought about the river's descent from heaven to Earth (see box, page 51).

But the place that attracts most pilgrims is Varanasi, a city celebrated by Jains and Buddhists alike as the major holy place of India. Here the water symbolizes Shiva's power, and every year over a million Hindus journey to bathe in it, cleansing themselves of the *karma* of previous lives and ensuring themselves an auspicious rebirth. And many come to make their final journey from its banks, to die and have their ashes cast into the water, dissolving into the distant world beyond.

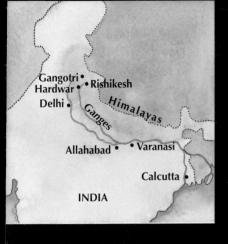

INDIA

Left: After the decline of the Indus Valley civilizations, the Ganges became the focus for subsequent Indian cultures. The Gangetic plains were the first part of the country to be overrun by Muslim invaders in the 13th century, as the fertile land offered immediate rewards far greater than more central areas. The lower Ganges remains the country's most important rice-growing area, while wheat flourishes by the river's higher reaches.

Below: Hindu holy sites afford the pilgrim *darshan*—the experience of the divine achieved through seeing, and being seen by, the image of God. With the Ganges, the object of devotion is the water itself, the energy of Shiva, offering physical and spiritual cleansing. The river is also a place of transition: the goddess Ganga is often shown as door-keeper to one of the four *gopuras,* the gateways between this world and the next.

Right: The story of the descent of the Ganges is told in this 7th-century stone carving at Mahabalipuram, Tamil Nadu. As the water crashed to Earth, the ashes of the Sagaras came to life and ascended to heaven. Today's cremations at Varanasi repeat their journey.

Left: The river is personified in the form of the goddess Ganga, shown here in a 12th-century stone statue from Mahanad, in Bengal. She was the daughter of the mountain god Himalaya and, having been first married to Vishnu, became one of the wives of Shiva.

Left: The city of Varanasi is crowded with temples, the greatest of which, Vishvanatha, celebrates Shiva as Lord of the Universe. The gilded spire and dome were built in 1835, but the temple itself dates from the late 18th century. The original, built in 1001, was razed by the Mughal emperor Aurangzeb, who replaced it with a mosque. There is also a Buddhist presence: 6.2 miles (10 kilometers) away is Sarnath, one of Buddhism's spiritual homes.

Below: Throughout the year, the city's flower market remains a colorful focus for pilgrims and traders alike. Bright bunches of marigolds dominate the streets, since yellow and orange symbolize purity and holiness. The colors are also associated with Shiva.

Right: Varanasi and its river are a *mokshadvara*, or door to liberation, so to have one's funeral here is to ensure a direct path to heaven. Thousands come to the city to commit the ashes of dead relatives to the water. Cremations should occur before sunset on the day of death.

Left: There has been a city on this site since well before the Christian era. Buddha gave his first sermon here in about 500 BCE, when the city, then known as Kashi, "City of Light," was already renowned as one of the oldest on Earth.

THE MANY MASKS OF A GENTLE GOD

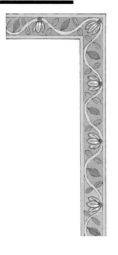

The followers of Vishnu emphasize their god's gentleness and compassion. The supreme deity, they say, has no need to assert his supremacy over others. As his ten incarnations show, Vishnu does use violence to defeat evil, but when not fighting demons, he is gentle and approachable. His seventh incarnation, Rama (see pages 62–69), is a courageous warrior, but one renowned for his virtue and kindness. Even when he comes into conflict with other gods, Vishnu takes a nonviolent role. When living with the cowherds, Krishna, Vishnu's eighth incarnation, angered Indra by persuading his companions to abandon their propitiatory sacrifices to him. When Indra summoned up a terrifying rainstorm in retaliation, Krishna merely lifted the great mountain Govardhana above his head to protect the cowherds. Indra's fury soon abated, and he came down to Earth and paid homage to the divine Krishna.

Like Shiva, Vishnu embodies many gods. He is partly a sun god who, in the *Rig Veda,* scales the universe with three great steps. He was later associated with Purusha, who in the same book is sacrificed in the creation of the universe (see page 28). Vishnu was also identified with Vasudeva, a popular hero worshipped as a god in western India in around the second century BCE. Krishna's pastoral youth appears to be based on the mythical exploits of a god of the fields and groves who, like Krishna, made enchanting music with his flute. Some scholars argue that Vishnu's origins were as a pre-Aryan deity who was absorbed into the Aryan pantheon and then into Hinduism.

But, to some, Vishnu's various aspects are just different ways of approaching *brahman.* The central characteristic of Vaishnavite cults is the practice of *bhakti,* devotion to god as Vishnu, and it is one of the main lessons taught by Krishna in the *Bhagavad Gita* that devotional worship should supersede the old ways of sacrificial ritual or austere ascetic rites. But, as he tells Arjuna on the eve of the battle of Kurukshetra at the climax of the *Mahabharata,* all ways lead to Vishnu, and unity with him is the sole purpose of earthly life.

Left: A 15th-century statue of Narasimha, from Vijayanagara. This man-lion was Vishnu's fourth incarnation.

Opposite: Vishnu sits surrounded by his 10 avatars in an 18th-century painting from Jaipur, Rajasthan. His incarnations included animals, like the boar and tortoise, men, like Rama, and even a god, Krishna. He was also Buddha, but has yet to appear as Kalki, the restorer of purity and peace at the end of time.

57

The Great Preserver

Images of Vishnu in his ten incarnations or avatars are popular with Hindus, and he is widely worshipped in these different forms. The concept of his many incarnations has allowed followers of Vishnu to incorporate into their worship a wide range of pre-Aryan heroes and popular deities.

This 18th-century wooden figure shows Vishnu in his first incarnation as the fish-man Matsya. He saved Manu from the flood and then killed the demon Hayagriva.

Vishnu took some terrifying forms in the course of his incarnations on Earth. But in every case it was his overriding role as protector and preserver that inspired him to take flesh as an animal or human. He came to Earth to avert a catastrophe or right a wrong—and so maintain *dharma*.

The number and kind of Vishnu's manifestations varies in different sources and is said by some to be beyond counting, but the generally accepted number of the principal incarnations is ten. The avatars reflect the evolution of life on Earth—beginning in the waters as a fish and ending at the terrible end of the current age of disintegration with Kalki the Destroyer.

The Animal Avatars

At the dawn of the present age, Vishnu was incarnated as Matsya the fish-man. He came to save Manu Vaivasvata, the father of the human race, from a great deluge and to kill a demon named Hayagriva ("Horseneck") that had stolen the sacred *Veda* from Brahma while the god slumbered.

Matsya first appeared to Manu as a tiny fish in a handful of water that Manu had scooped up to perform his early morning devotions. As he watched, the fish grew. Manu put it in a jug, but still it grew. He transferred it to a large bowl, but it continued growing until he put it in the sea. Then the fish spoke, warning Manu that at the end of seven days a great flood would cover the land, and that he must build a ship, taking on board the religious sages, his family, animals and plant seeds. He should tie the boat to a horn on Matsya's back, and Matsya would tow them all to safety.

When the flood came, Manu did as he was told, and the fish's prophecy came true. Using the snake Sesa, Manu tied the boat to the fish's horn, and the fish towed Manu to a high Himalayan peak, where he and his companions waited for the flood to subside. Then Matsya killed the demon Hayagriva and took the *Veda* back to Brahma.

In his second incarnation, as Kurma the tortoise, Vishnu helped the gods and demons recover the *amrita* from the Ocean of Milk (see box, page 38). The *amrita* and certain other sacred objects had been lost when the universe was reduced to chaos at the end of a previous age, and Vishnu came to Earth in order to help recover them.

The gods and demons used Mount Mandara as a churning stick to stir up the ocean, and Kurma swam to the seabed so that they could rest the heavy mountain on his back while they did so. The churning was a great success, and as well as the *amrita,* several other treasures were recovered from the ocean, including the goddess Lakshmi, or Sri, who became Vishnu's wife; Chandra, the moon; and the astonishing white elephant Airavata, who became Indra's mount.

Scholars believe that pre-Aryan Indians worshipped the tortoise. They are thought to have seen the animal as an embodiment of the universe—with the upper shell standing for the sky above and the lower shell standing for the Earth below, while the soft body of the tortoise in between represented the atmosphere.

Vishnu's third avatar was Varaha the boar, who rescued the Earth from the floor of the primordial ocean, where the demon Hiranyaksha ("Golden Eye") had taken it. The demon had performed great austerities, which had persuaded Brahma to grant his plea that no man, animal or god would be able to kill him. Delighting in his invulnerability, Hiranyaksha ran riot, attacking men and women, provoking the gods, stealing the

Body of the Gods

Images of Vishnu often show him with dark blue skin, representing endlessness or infinity.

Vishnu is usually shown either seated on a lotus or lying on the 100-headed serpent Ananta, afloat on the cosmic waters. He takes this form after the universe has been destroyed and before it is recreated (see page 33).

One of his four hands is empty, its open palm representing generosity. In another, he holds a discus, which symbolizes the sun, the source of life. The discus is sometimes replaced by a wheel, standing for the cycle of life, death and rebirth.

In the third hand, he holds a conch shell, the source of the five elements. His fourth hand holds a lotus, signifying creative power or sometimes a club, standing for time. The god wears a golden garment that signifies the holy *Vedas* or scriptures. He also carries a bow and a sword. As the great preserver, Vishnu flies on the back of the fearless golden-breasted bird Garuda. His consort is Lakshmi, goddess of prosperity and wealth.

An early 19th-century painting of Vishnu as Visvarupa, in whom he represents the universe and all the Hindu gods.

A 19th-century bronze statue of Vishnu as Kalki, from south India. In this, his final incarnation, Vishnu will descend to the Earth at the end of time to restore moral order. The figure has four hands holding the attributes of Vishnu: a wheel, symbol of the cycle of life; a conch shell, the source of all things; the lotus flower, creativity; and the club, time.

sacred scriptures from Brahma and as a final insult, hurling the Earth to the bottom of the ocean.

But the demon had one vulnerable point: when dealing with Brahma, Hiranyaksha had had to recite the names of the animals that would be unable to hurt him—and he had forgotten the boar. Vishnu therefore assumed the form of a vast boar with a roar louder than Indra's thunder and flaming eyes brighter than lightning. Shining like the sun, Varaha the boar swam to the seabed, killed Hiranyaksha and rescued the Earth, setting it floating once more on the surface. Vishnu incarnated as the man-lion Narasimha to kill yet another demon. Hiranyakasipu was the brother of Hiranyaksha, and he, too, stole the Earth and won a similar boon from Brahma. In his case, no god, man, or animal could kill him, by night or day, neither inside a building nor under the open heavens.

Like his brother, Hiranyakasipu was driven to wild behavior by the knowledge that he was immortal. He set himself up as the one god and banned all other forms of worship. But his own son, Prahlada, was a devoted Vaishnavite and refused to abandon his god. This drove his father into a frenzy of rage, and—snorting and spitting—he vowed to kill his son. He sent snakes and elephants to attack Prahlada, but the young man was unharmed. In fact, no matter what the demon tried, his son always walked away unhurt.

Again and again, Prahlada refused to abandon Vishnu and insisted that the god was all around them. At dusk one day Hiranyakasipu angrily asked Prahlada whether Vishnu was inside a pillar at the doorway of his temple. Prahlada replied that he certainly was; and Hiranyakasipu, yelling that he would murder the god there and then if he could, kicked the pillar. Narasimha-Vishnu then stepped out of the pillar and ripped the demon king to pieces. He did not break the terms of Brahma's boon as it was dusk—neither day nor night; he was in the temple doorway—neither inside nor outside; and he had taken the form of a man-lion—neither god, man nor animal.

Vishnu's later avatars saw him take human form. When the gods lost their heavenly kingdom to the ambitious Earthly king, Bali, Vishnu became Vamana the dwarf, son of Aditi and the sage Kasyapa, to win it back. Vamana, exploiting Bali's

This 5th-century sandstone figure from Maharashtra shows Vishnu as Vamana the dwarf. When King Bali offered him as much land as he could cross in three paces, Vamana grew to a great size and took Bali's entire kingdom.

reputation for kindness, asked the king for as much land as he could cover with three strides. Bali agreed happily but then watched in horror as Vamana expanded in size and strode across his land, taking all except the underworld, Patala, which he gave to Bali in recognition of his kindness in granting the boon. Vishnu then came to Earth as Parasurama, son of a *brahmin* named Jamadagni. This was at a time when the *kshatriya*, or warrior-king class, was abusing its position and tyrannizing other people including the *brahmin* priests. Vishnu's aim was to restore order and bring the priests back to an eminent position.

The seventh incarnation was Ramacandra, righteous and courageous hero of the *Ramayana* epic (see pages 62–69). The eighth was Krishna, cowherd, teacher and prince (see page 70). The ninth was Gautama Buddha, at the start of the present age. Some say that Vishnu's purpose was to mislead the wicked and arrogant by diverting their attention from the sacred scriptures, but others suggest that he took the form of the Buddha out of a desire to ease the sufferings of animals and to stop religious sacrifices. Clearly Buddhism was a rival to Hinduism. The Buddha was incorporated into the worship of Vishnu, either to demean Buddhism and assert Hinduism's superiority or to absorb the faith into the Hindu mainstream in the same way that many Vedic and pre-Aryan deities had become Hindu gods.

The tenth and final incarnation, Kalki, has yet to occur. At the end of the present age, Vishnu will appear clasping a burning sword and mounted on a powerful white steed. The world will then be destroyed before a new creation. This idea may have been influenced by the Buddhist doctrine of the Maitreya Buddha. In the *Mahabharata*, Kalki is a *brahmin* who will judge men and women, rewarding the good and punishing the evil. In southern India, Kalki is shown as a horse—probably a survival of a pre-Aryan horse-worshipping cult.

Prince Rama and the Demon King

Vishnu took the form of the handsome warrior prince Rama to save the Earth from the wicked demon king Ravana. He combined gentleness and virtue with courage, and physical beauty with vast strength, making him one of the most enduring Hindu heroes.

The tale of Rama's heroic exploits is told in the Sanskrit epic the *Ramayana*, which is still performed in India by professional storytellers. The epic was fashioned into its surviving form over the years between c. 200 BCE and 200 CE. It is said to be the work of a hermit-poet named Valmiki, who appears at the end of the narrative, although in reality it has evolved over generations.

The *Ramayana* was originally an account of the warring adventures of a historical tribal chief named Rama. As in the poem, he was son of King Dasaratha, who lived sometime between 1000 and 700 BCE. It became increasingly devotional over the years, as passages on gods and religious ritual were added. The first of its seven books, which scholars have shown to be among the last composed, claims that Rama is an incarnation of Vishnu.

The lovers Rama and Sita as seen by the Deccan artist Rahim Deccani, who painted this scene on the side of a lacquered jewel casket, *c.* 1660. Sita was an incarnation of Vishnu's consort Lakshmi, who later became Krishna's lover Radha as well.

An Unconquerable Demon

Ravana, the fearsome ten-headed demon king of the island of Sri Lanka, was all-powerful. One day, filled with the heat of *tapas* after great austerities and penances, he asked Brahma to make him so strong that no god or demon could beat him in combat, and Brahma was forced to grant this boon. Like many demons before him, once Ravana knew he was invulnerable, he ran riot – defiling priestly sacrifices and even capturing the wind god Vayu and Agni, god of the sacrificial fire. Indra and the other gods begged Brahma to help them, and he took them to see Vishnu.

When the lesser gods explained why they were distressed, the great protector calmed them and said that the terms of Ravana's boon did not protect him from men or apes. The gods should descend and take the form of apes, he said, while he would be born in the form of four princes.

Meanwhile, Dasaratha, the king of Kosala in northern India, longed for a son and performed a horse sacrifice to propitiate the gods. A fine black stallion was released, accompanied by a priest, and wandered for a full year to fulfil the rules of ritual sacrifice. When it returned, priests chanted mantras while Kausalya, the king's principal wife, killed it herself with a sacred sword.

In time, each of Dasaratha's three wives gave birth to sons, and all of them were incarnations of Vishnu. The first to be born was Rama, Kausalya's child, who had half of Vishnu's nature. The second wife, Kaikeyi, was the mother of Bharata, who was filled with one quarter of the great god's spirit. The third wife, Sumitra, then gave birth to twins, called Lakshmana and Satrughna, each of whom had one eighth of Vishnu's being.

As the boys grew up, they acquired great learning, wisdom and military prowess. But Rama was the most beautiful of the children. Rama and his half-brother Lakshmana were inseparable, and loved to play and learn together. When Rama was sixteen, he helped the great sage Vishwamitra dispatch demons that had been interfering with religious sacrifices. As a result, he was granted heavenly weapons with which to fight. The sage also took Rama and Lakshmana to the kingdom of Mithila to witness a sacrifice being made by Janaka, king of that realm.

Janaka had a beautiful and gentle daughter, and princes came from far and wide seeking her hand. She was an incarnation of the goddess Lakshmi, Vishnu's heavenly consort, and she took the name Sita ("Furrow") because she was born

Rama appears with pendulous ears adorned with jewelry in a 13th-century bronze statue from southern India. This popular hero and his wife Sita together embody incorruptibility and fidelity.

63

from the earth of a ploughed field. After his daughter, the king's most prized possession was a bow that had once belonged to the great god Shiva. It was so vast that mere mortals could not lift it, and it could only be moved on an eight-wheeled iron chariot pulled by many strong men.

When Rama and Lakshmana came to court, Janaka greeted them courteously. They asked to see the bow, and when it was wheeled into their presence, Janaka declared that any man able to bend Shiva's bow could marry Sita. Rama picked up the bow, strung it and with his great strength bent it so far that it snapped in the middle. As it broke, it made a sound like thunder, and the mountains and fields seemed to tremble.

Janaka declared that Rama was surely without equal and was worthy of Sita's hand in marriage. Rama and Sita were married and Dasaratha soon declared that he would pass the throne to Rama. Everyone rejoiced, welcoming his decision.

Lakshmana looses an arrow aimed at the demon Surpanakha who, disguised as a beautiful woman, had tried to woo both him and the faithful Rama, and so undermine the purity of their souls. From a 17th-century Rajput dynasty watercolor.

But on the day before the coronation, one of Queen Kaikeyi's servants poisoned this happy atmosphere by stirring up resentment in Kaikeyi that Rama, and not her own son Bharata, was to be king. Many years before, Kaikeyi had cured Dasaratha when he was close to death after being hurt by a demon, and the king had promised her two boons. Now Kaikeyi went to see Dasaratha and reminded him of his promise.

The king, mindful of how she had saved his life, said again that he would give her whatever she desired. So Kaikeyi demanded that the king send Rama into exile for fourteen years and give his throne to Bharata.

Dasaratha was horrified. Kaikeyi had tricked him. The king rolled his eyes and sighed deeply, for he had to keep his word and grant her wish. But when Dasaratha told Rama, the prince remained calm: he was happy to obey his father's orders. Dasaratha wept and, as the news spread, grief swept through the land. Sita insisted on going with Rama into exile, and although he tried to dissuade her, she would not give way. Lakshmana was also determined to accompany his beloved brother Rama. And so, on that very day, Rama, Sita and Lakshmana set out for the forest.

Within a few days, Dasaratha, who could not bear the loss of his eldest son, died of a broken heart. When Bharata returned to Ayodhya and discovered what had happened, he cursed his mother. He did not want to profit from his brother's loss. He considered striking her down, but he realized that even after what she had done, he must still honor her as his mother.

Bharata went to the forest to ask Rama to return and take up his rightful position, but Rama would not go against his father's decree. Bharata gave Rama a pair of precious sandals decorated with gold, but Rama refused them, saying he would live a simple hermit's life wearing his hair matted like a sage and a rough suit of bark. Bharata returned sadly to Ayodhya and placed the sandals on his throne to signify that his realm rightfully belonged to his elder brother.

The exiles travelled southward, and from time to time helped sages who were troubled by demons, until they settled peacefully in a hut on the banks of the Godavari River in southern India. Years went by, and Lakshmana and Sita were a great comfort to Rama. The time came when just six months of their fourteen-year exile remained.

Then one day a hideous demon-woman named Surpanakha happened to pass through that corner of the forest. When she saw Rama's handsome lotus-blue body,

she was filled with longing for him. Surpanakha transformed herself into a beautiful maiden to approach the prince. She flattered him and offered him the rule of a great kingdom if he would come with her. Rama declared that nothing could tempt him to abandon Sita but that Lakshmana was in need of a wife. So the demon tested her wiles on Lakshmana, but he did not treat her seriously. At once she flew into a rage and tried to attack Sita. Rama pushed her roughly back, and Lakshmana drew his bow and shot her in the nose and ears. The screaming Surpanakha fled.

One of Surpanakha's brothers was the demon Khara, and she flew to him, demanding revenge. Khara acted at once, marching into the forest at the head of an army of 14,000 demons. But Rama killed the entire army and its leader in a single day. So Surpanakha fled to another of her brothers, the demon Ravana, king of the island of Sri Lanka. She told him of Rama's violence against their fellow demons and advised the king that the best way to hurt Rama would be to take away his beloved Sita.

The king and another demon brother, Maricha, at once travelled to the forest, hauled through the air in Ravana's great chariot by a team of panting demons. Maricha took the form of a breathtakingly beautiful deer and wandered up to the fair Sita as she was gathering wild flowers from the carpet of blooms on the forest floor.

This Sindhi sword, with a hilt of silver and gold and a blade of Iranian steel, dates from the 17th century. The warlike endeavors of the heroes of the *Ramayana* and the *Mahabharata* recall the battles fought by the Aryan warriors of the pre-Vedic age who defined the gods of Hindu India. Victory in battle symbolized a triumph of good over evil.

65

Rama's greatest desire was to make Sita happy, and when she said that she longed to possess the deer's soft hide, he seized his bow and went after the animal. It took a long chase, but Rama finally shot the deer and the demon leapt out of its body. It imitated Rama's voice and sent up a great cry, calling to Lakshmana and Sita for help.

Back at the hut, Rama's companions heard the cry, and Sita begged Lakshmana to go and help him. At first he refused, for he was only too aware that it might be the work of bewitching demons who could take many forms and imitate any voice. But Sita was so upset that eventually Lakshmana went off to investigate. As soon as Lakshmana had gone, Ravana disguised himself as a sage and approached Sita through the trees.

Sita greeted him courteously and told him the story of her wandering with Rama. Then Ravana told her who he truly was and tried to tempt her to abandon Rama and come with him to Sri Lanka as his glorious queen. Sita looked at him dismissively. Rama was her lion, she said, and Ravana a mere jackal who should turn tail and flee.

Ravana, smarting, reverted to his true form as king of the demons, seized her and flew off towards Sri Lanka. Sita screamed for Rama and Lakshmana to help her, to no avail. But Jatayus, king of the vultures, was asleep on a nearby peak and did hear her cries. He flew straight at Ravana, like one of the great Indra's thunderbolts.

In the raging battle that followed, Jatayus smashed Ravana's chariot and killed his horses, but Ravana dealt Jatayus a mortal blow with his sword. The demon king then took Sita and flew high beyond the vulture's range and on towards Sri Lanka. As they passed over a place named the Mountain of the Apes, Sita, still calling forlornly to Rama and Lakshmana, threw down her jewelry. Far below, the apes saw her, heard her cries and found the ornaments she had dropped.

Jatayus, king of the vultures, tries in vain to rescue Rama's wife Sita from the clutches of Ravana, the demon king, in an illustration of the *Ramayana, c.* 1760. Before he died, however, Jatayus was able to tell Rama what had happened to his wife.

In the forest, Rama was overcome with grief when he found Sita gone from the hut. He hung his head: Sita was his life, he said, and without her he had nothing. All night he and Lakshmana wandered through the forest, searching for her in vain.

When dawn broke, they found the vulture Jatayus where he had fallen to the ground after being hurt by Ravana. He told the brothers how Sita had been carried off to the south by the demon. Then he died in Rama's arms. Rama respectfully burned the vulture's body, and its soul flew up to Vishnu's heaven.

Then Rama and Lakshmana travelled on toward the south, but encountered a horrid demon blocking their path. They fought for all they were worth and succeeded in slicing through the monster's arms. Lying twitching on the ground before them, the demon begged the brothers to burn his body, in return for which, he promised, he would tell them how to recover Sita.

They did as he asked, and the demon was transformed into a glorious celestial being named Kabandha. He told them that Sita had been carried off by Ravana and advised them to seek the help of the monkey king, Sugriva, who lived high up in the mountains of southern India.

Land of the Apes

The brothers bid Kabandha farewell and went in search of Sugriva. The king greeted them and showed them the ornaments he had seen thrown from the sky. They filled Rama with sadness and fuelled his desire for revenge. But, with the coming of the rainy season, he was condemned to wait with Lakshmana as Sugriva's guest.

Far away in Sri Lanka, Ravana would not rest from his attempts to seduce Sita. But she was always loyal to her husband. She thought only of Rama and took pleasure in nothing.

When the rainy season came to an end, Rama asked Sugriva to help him in his search for Sita. The monkey king agreed readily, and assembled a great army of bears, apes and monkeys for the campaign. One of the apes was Hanuman, son of the wind god Vayu. He had many powers, including the ability to fly, and he soared across the sea from India to Sri Lanka in his search for Sita.

Hanuman found the princess in Ravana's palace and told her of the planned attack. She gave him a ring to carry to Rama as a sign of her faithfulness and undying love. Hanuman left her, but before he returned across the water, he set about making mischief in Ravana's city. He killed many soldiers and destroyed many fine buildings but finally was captured. Ravana decided to injure the ape and then send him back in order to frighten the monkey army. He ordered that cloths soaked in oil be tied around Hanuman's tail and set alight. But the moment this was done, Hanuman escaped and ran through the city setting fire to many buildings. Then he flew back to Rama and told him that he had found the princess.

Rama and Lakshmana rejoiced loudly at the news. Then they led their army southwards and set up camp on the Indian shore opposite Sri Lanka. Here they were joined by Ravana's brother Vibhishana, who had been banished from the demon king's court because he had tried to persuade Ravana to make peace with Rama. But there was no way across the waters for this great army.

Rama then found the craftsman Nala among the monkey hosts. He was an incarnation of the divine artisan Visvakarman or Tvastr (see box, page 49), and knew how to build a bridge across the straits. In just five days, Nala built a line of rocky islands to link India and Sri Lanka – which can still be seen today. Before setting out on the dangerous expedition, Rama won the favor of Shiva by setting up and worshipping an image of Shiva's all-powerful *lingam*.

Then the army formed into lines. Rama climbed on to Hanuman's back, Lakshmana clambered on to the back of another monkey, Angada, and they made the crossing, leaping from one island to the next. They reached Sri Lanka and set up their camp opposite Ravana's city. Out from the city came the demon army, mounted on lions, wolves, elephants and other animals amid a cacophony of thumping drums and blaring horns.

67

Hanuman the Monkey-King

Rama's loyal general Hanuman was a golden-bodied monkey with a ruby-red face and a devastating roar. Strong enough to lift a mountain, he also had magical powers to shift shape or become invisible. He could also fly because his father was the wind god Vayu.

Hanuman was born to help Rama in his battle against Ravana, for Vishnu had told the gods to father a race of monkeys to fight the demons.

When King Dasaratha performed his horse sacrifice in the hope of becoming a father, he distributed cakes to his three wives. But the youngest, Kaikeyi, refused hers because she had been handed it last—and a bird carried it away. Deep in the forest the bird dropped it, and Vayu with his soft breath blew it into the hand of a monkey named Anjana. She held the cake for a few moments, turning it over and over in wonder, and then Shiva himself appeared to her, ordering her to consume it. As she ate it, she became pregnant with Rama's loyal friend.

Hanuman had the great appetite of a god, and Anjana was unable to pacify his extreme hunger. When Hanuman one day caught sight of the sun in the sky, he mistook it for a golden fruit, and using his father's power of flight, he jumped up to seize it. The sun fled, but Hanuman followed. In Swarga, Indra's heaven, Indra attacked the monkey with a thunderbolt, and Hanuman fell back to Earth. But Vayu saw what had happened, and in a rage for revenge he swept into the bodies of all the gods, torturing them with burning indigestion. Then Indra made peace with Vayu, and the wind god persuaded him to grant Hanuman the ultimate boon of immortality.

In other versions of the Hanuman myth, Rama made the monkey general immortal as a sign of his gratitude. After their victory over Ravana, Rama offered Hanuman anything he wished, and the monkey asked only to live for as long as men talked of Rama – and Rama's fame will live forever.

Hanuman, the monkey god, adorns a silver altarpiece from the Chamundi Hills, in Mysore. The monkey's devotion to Rama was such that he became revered as a god in his own right.

According to the legends of the *Ramayana*, the islands between Sri Lanka and the Indian mainland were made by the craftsman Nala to form a bridge so that Rama could cross the water and bring his armies to the gates of Ravana's stronghold.

The battle raged for three whole days, until the climax when Ravana and Rama fought mightily against one another. Rama eventually seized a divine weapon provided by Brahma himself, and with this he shattered the iron heart of the demon king. Ravana swooned, fell down and died. Rama's task was accomplished.

The remnants of the demon army fled, and Rama declared Vibhishana king of Sri Lanka. Then he gave orders that Sita should be brought to him. She was carried to him across the flower-strewn plain crying softly with happiness. But Rama treated her coldly. She had been in Ravana's palace, and shame had attached itself to her since it was possible that she had been unfaithful.

Sita protested her innocence, but Rama said nothing. Then Sita asked Lakshmana to build a funeral pyre and, to demonstrate that she was free of sin, she flung herself into the flames. Rama felt deep regret, for he realized that she was indeed innocent. But in that instant the flames parted, and Agni the fire god came forth carrying Sita. He gave her to Rama, saying that she was free of guilt. Then Rama and Sita embraced joyfully.

They went quickly back to Ayodhya, where Bharata was overjoyed to see them and delighted to return the throne to his brother. Rama was crowned king. But over the weeks and months that followed, the people of the city began to whisper against Sita again, doubting her innocence. Rama felt driven to appease them, although he loved Sita still, and he sent her into forest exile.

Sita found shelter with Valmiki—the poet of the *Ramayana*—and gave birth to twin boys, Lava and Kusa. Years later the boys returned to Ayodhya, and Rama recognized them. He sent messengers asking Sita to return, and when she did, he asked her one last time to swear her innocence. But she was weary of so many doubts cast on her fidelity, which had in truth never wavered for an instant. She called on the Earth—her mother, for she was born of a furrow—to reclaim her as a final proof that she had been faithful, and she was swallowed into the ground according to her wish.

Rama was maddened by sorrow, for he had lost his true consort. He continued to mourn her for the rest of his days and, shortly after, abdicated in favor of his sons. At the appointed time, Garuda, Vishnu's faithful mount, descended to Ayodhya for him, and Rama rose to Heaven. There, once again in the form of Vishnu, he found Sita in the form of Lakshmi, and they were at last reunited in glorious and eternal happiness.

69

A Divine Shepherd Boy

Many stories are told of Vishnu's eighth incarnation as the princely shepherd boy Krishna. As a child, he defeated countless demons before developing into a good-natured youth, renowned as a lover of country women and the pleasures of music and dancing.

Vishnu's principal purpose in taking the form of Krishna was to defeat the demon Kamsa. This evil prince ruled the land of the Yadavas by the banks of the great Yamuna River in northern India. He had seized his stepfather's throne, outlawed the cult of Vishnu and proceeded continually to wield his power abusively.

The Earth herself begged the gods to rid her of Kamsa. So Brahma led the deities to see the great lord and protector Vishnu, who agreed to come down again to save the Earth.

On Earth, Devaki, beautiful cousin of the wicked King Kamsa, was preparing to marry a man named Vasudeva. But a soothsayer warned the king that, according to prophecy, the fruit of Devaki's womb would one day kill him. Kamsa wanted to strike his cousin dead, but a better plan occurred to him. He would allow her to live in the palace where he could keep a close watch on her, and he would instantly kill each child she bore.

Devaki gave birth to six sons, and each one died at the heartless Kamsa's hands. Now Vasudeva had another fair wife, Rohini, and he sent her away from the dangerous intrigues at court to stay with a cowherd named Nanda. When Devaki became pregnant a seventh time, Vishnu used his great powers to transfer the embryo to Rohini's womb. She gave birth safely to the child, who grew up to be Krishna's elder brother Balarama. They told King Kamsa that Devaki had lost her baby before her time.

In due course, Devaki became pregnant again. Kamsa was suspicious, and hatred swelled within him when he saw the physical signs indicating that Devaki was about to give birth once more. This time he cast Devaki and her husband into prison and set guards to watch them day and night. The child in Devaki's womb was Krishna. Far away in the countryside, Nanda's wife, Yashoda, was pregnant, too; her child was the goddess Devi.

One night beneath a waning moon, as thunder cracked and monsoon rains deluged the thirsty countryside, Yashoda and Devaki both gave birth.

Krishna, with Devi's mother Yashoda, from a Kangara watercolor, c. 1800. After King Kamsa had slaughtered all Devaki's offspring, Vishnu ensured that her son Krishna was mothered by Yashoda, who loved the child as her own son.

Mountains trembled, fires flared up and for an instant, the rain gave way to a soft falling of petals as Krishna was born.

Then Vasudeva heard a heavenly voice, which told him to take the newborn boy to the safety of Nanda's house and switch it with the newly delivered female baby he would find there. He feared that it was impossible, for the prison doors were locked, and he knew that armed guards stood at attention outside. But he went ahead as he had been ordered, and when he came to the door he found it open; outside the guards were snoring softly. Finding a threshing basket, he hid the child and set off for Nanda's home, where he swapped the babies as instructed and took the girl back to the palace. He laid her on Devaki's chest, which moved softly up and down as she slept. Then he went to King Kamsa's chambers and told him that Devaki had given birth to a girl. Kamsa stormed down to the prison cell, picked up the child and hurled it on to the floor. But this time the baby did not scream in pain. Even before it hit the ground it was lifeless as a carcass, while above it rose a tall woman in celestial robes of blue and

The Slaying of Putana

Even as a baby, Krishna had an awesome power that revealed his status as the great god Vishnu. On one occasion, he defeated the hideous demon Putana who had been sent by King Kamsa to kill him.

Putana ("Stinking") made her way to Nanda's home. Her natural form was so hideous that she transformed herself into a beautiful young woman before knocking on the door. Krishna's stepmother Yashoda welcomed her, and Putana said she had heard that Yashoda was looking for a nurse for her son. It was true, Yashoda said, and the woman seemed so pleasant that she allowed her to stay.

One day Yashoda was unwell and took to her bed, and Putana saw her chance. When Krishna woke and began to cry for a feed, Putana took him on her lap and offered him her breast, which she had rubbed with poison. But as Krishna fed, he grew stronger and stronger. Putana began to scream and tried desperately to pull Krishna away. But he clung on with his gums and did not stop sucking until she lay dead on the floor in her original, terrible form.

Putana, the hideous monster, transforms herself into a beautiful woman in order to gain entrance to Nanda's house and kill the divine child, Krishna.

gold, with flowing locks and sweet-smelling garlands around her neck. She simply told the king that she was not the one he was looking for. Then he saw that she was a goddess, and as she rose to Heaven, she promised that when the end of his life came she would be there to glory in his extinction.

Kamsa turned in fury and roared that no one could outwit him. That night he ordered that all the male children in the kingdom were to be killed. But Krishna escaped, for Nanda, Yashoda and Balarama, his brother, fled with him to safety.

When the killing was over, they returned to their country home and threw a party to celebrate Krishna's birth. The *brahmins* who attended the celebration saw great things in the baby. They said he would bring wealth to the kingdom and would be an implacable enemy of demons. And so it proved.

Before he was even one year old, Krishna saw off a host of demon attacks. Putana, a hideous demoness, tried to poison him, but he got the better of her (see box, page 71). Another, Saktasura, tried to crush Krishna by overturning a cart he was lying on, but the baby showed he had the strength of a god by flipping the cart over and crushing the demon.

Krishna is seen as the most important avatar of Vishnu, and he is worshipped as a god in his own right. His life is fully described in the ninth-century CE *Bhagavata Purana*. In addition, the much earlier *Harivamsa*, a lengthy section of the *Mahabharata* epic, is largely dedicated to his childhood and youth. Many of these tales are probably derived from non-Aryan southern Indian stories about countryside deities. But other parts of his life story are almost certainly based on the exploits of a historical tribal hero of the Yadava people in northern India.

Krishna repeatedly proved his mastery of demons. One day, when he was a little older and his child's body was hardening into that of a man, the god and his friends were wandering on the banks of the Yamuna River. In that part the river was inhabited by a fearsome five-headed serpent, Kaliya, who had poisoned the waters. Everybody knew this, but the day was searingly hot, and the cowherds were confused by the heat and desperate for a drink, so they threw themselves down on the bank and took a long draught.

The poison was so powerful that instant death seized them all, except Krishna. He stood sadly gazing at his mortal friends, and the power of his gaze was such that just by looking at them, he brought them back to life. Then Krishna remembered that the waters had been poisoned by Kaliya, and he dived into the river to tame the serpent. Kaliya rose up angrily and grasped Krishna in his strong coils. But Krishna smashed two of the serpent's heads with his bare arms. Then he leaped onto the serpent's remaining three heads and danced on them, crushing them utterly.

Kaliya sank down, defeated once and for all. Blood poured from his mouth, and in his soul he recognized Krishna's true identity and fell down and worshipped Vishnu. On the riverbank, the cowherds cheered. In some versions of the tale, Kaliya's wives came forth from the water and paid homage to Krishna and begged for their husband's life. Krishna relented, but he sent the snakes far away into the ocean. The poison disappeared when they left, and the waters of the Yamuna River became safe to drink, and as sweet to the taste as the gods' drink *amrita*. Krishna and his young friends played and sported in the river, their glad shouts ringing out in the summer evening.

Left: A bronze statue of Krishna as a child, overcoming the demon snake Kaliya, from Madras, *c.* 16th–17th century. His strength was challenged by demons throughout his childhood.

Right: Scenes from the life of Krishna, from a 20th-century painting on cotton. The shepherd boy is much favored by artists who portray him as both divine and touchingly human.

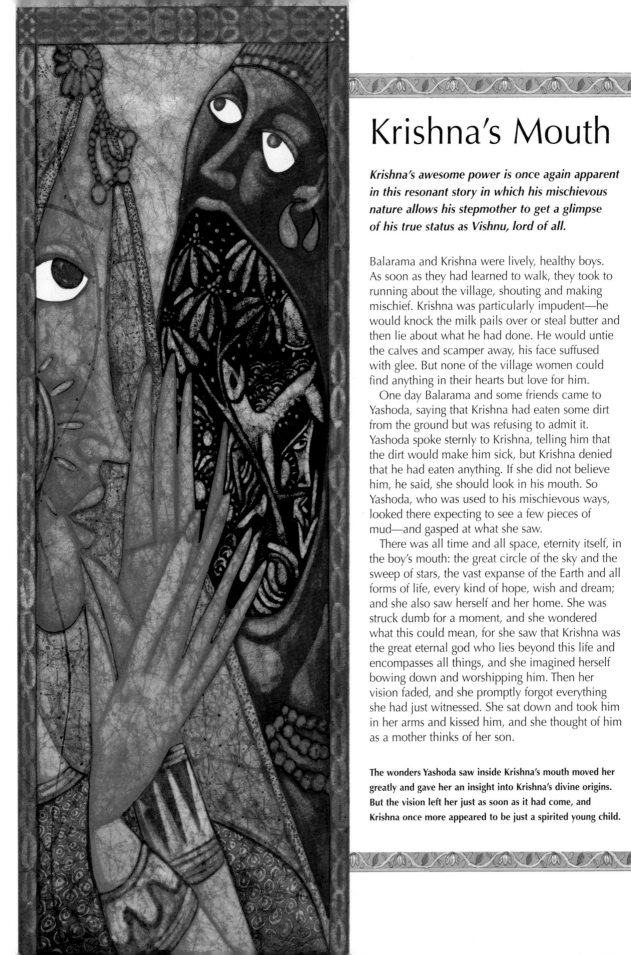

Krishna's Mouth

**Krishna's awesome power is once again apparent
in this resonant story in which his mischievous
nature allows his stepmother to get a glimpse
of his true status as Vishnu, lord of all.**

Balarama and Krishna were lively, healthy boys.
As soon as they had learned to walk, they took to
running about the village, shouting and making
mischief. Krishna was particularly impudent—he
would knock the milk pails over or steal butter and
then lie about what he had done. He would untie
the calves and scamper away, his face suffused
with glee. But none of the village women could
find anything in their hearts but love for him.

One day Balarama and some friends came to
Yashoda, saying that Krishna had eaten some dirt
from the ground but was refusing to admit it.
Yashoda spoke sternly to Krishna, telling him that
the dirt would make him sick, but Krishna denied
that he had eaten anything. If she did not believe
him, he said, she should look in his mouth. So
Yashoda, who was used to his mischievous ways,
looked there expecting to see a few pieces of
mud—and gasped at what she saw.

There was all time and all space, eternity itself, in
the boy's mouth: the great circle of the sky and the
sweep of stars, the vast expanse of the Earth and all
forms of life, every kind of hope, wish and dream;
and she also saw herself and her home. She was
struck dumb for a moment, and she wondered
what this could mean, for she saw that Krishna was
the great eternal god who lies beyond this life and
encompasses all things, and she imagined herself
bowing down and worshipping him. Then her
vision faded, and she promptly forgot everything
she had just witnessed. She sat down and took him
in her arms and kissed him, and she thought of him
as a mother thinks of her son.

**The wonders Yashoda saw inside Krishna's mouth moved her
greatly and gave her an insight into Krishna's divine origins.
But the vision left her just as soon as it had come, and
Krishna once more appeared to be just a spirited young child.**

Radha and Krishna

After his mischievous childhood, when the mothers in the village thought he could do no wrong, Krishna developed into a handsome and talented young man. His looks, good humor and entrancing music-making made him the favorite of all the young women.

All the young wives in the village had a common passion: Krishna, the good-looking son of Nanda. They made offerings of flowers, leaves, fruit and rice to the goddess Durga (a form of Devi, consort of Shiva) and each one prayed that she might become Krishna's lover. They all loved him equally, and it was no secret among them. Each morning they went to bathe in the river, and as soon as they were out of earshot of their husbands, they talked happily about their love.

Krishna was aware of the women's passion, and he was attracted by their beauty. One morning he even followed them and played a trick on them by hiding their clothes when they were bathing. But he had a favorite, Radha, who was married to the cowherd Ayanaghosa.

Krishna's love for Radha is a favorite subject of Indian poetry. The medieval lyric poem the *Gitagovinda* (see box, page 76) describes it in exquisite terms. Krishna and Radha meet and fall in love, they part and are then joyfully reconciled.

Radha is occasionally seen as Krishna's wife, but usually she is his mistress. Krishna later became a devoted husband with many wives. His favorite is said to have been Rukmini, with whom he eloped on the morning she was to marry the demon Sisupula. But Radha is remembered as his great romantic passion. Both Radha and Rukmini are said to be incarnations of Lakshmi, Vishnu's consort

Krishna's companion Radha swoons as her maidservant admonishes him on returning from seeing another lover. Watercolor from Basolili in the Punjab Hills, *c.*1660.

and goddess of prosperity and beauty. Lakshmi took human form to accompany Vishnu through all his incarnations. When he came to Earth as Rama, she took the form of his faithful wife, Sita (see pages 63–69).

After Krishna had toyed with the young wives by stealing their clothes, he promised to dance with them in the rainy season. When the time came, he crept away alone into the heart of the woods. The rains had passed, and it was a clear moonlit night, almost still. He sat for a while, and then he took his flute and played a delicate song.

75

In the village many of the young wives lay awake, restless because of their longing for Krishna. They heard the delicate melody he played and went quietly to find him. Krishna took pains to greet each of them individually, and when he made a lighthearted jest, their laughter rang out in the moonlight like temple bells.

Then the dance began, and the women found themselves floating on its sweet movements. Each swooned inwardly as she knew she had Krishna's full attention, for the shepherd boy used his divine magic to make it seem as if he were dancing intimately and intensely with each and every woman. But Krishna soon moved close to his beloved Radha and persuaded her to come away with him.

With Krishna gone, the other girls seemed to wake from their sweet dream, and they saw that they were alone, dancing foolishly in the forest without their dear lover. Many of them began to cry. Then one of them noticed that Radha was also missing, and they set off to find the couple, to ask Krishna to return to them.

A Pastoral Love Story

The Gitagovinda, a twelfth-century lyrical poem by Jayadeva, celebrates the love of Krishna and Radha and is a favorite among Vaishnavites.

Gitagovinda means in Sanskrit "Song of the Cowherd." It describes how the divine cowherd Krishna falls for Radha, but their mutual attraction is followed by a disagreement. After a passage of romantic agony and longing, they are at last reconciled. The poem focuses on the exquisite pain of separation for lovers.

The *Gitagovinda* is praised by scholars as a great literary work. Devotees see it as an inspired treatment of the relationship of a worshipper with his or her god. Followers of Vishnu become like Radha, forever in love with Krishna but also periodically separated from him. In the poem Radha is already married when she falls in love with Krishna, and her extramarital affair with him goes strongly against social convention. But her total love for Krishna and willingness to risk her reputation for him is an example for devotees who aspire to a similar love for their god.

The author Jayadeva was a *brahmin's* son, who was connected to the court of King Laksmanasena at Navadvipa. His poem was certainly the first work to focus on the romantic passion of Radha and Krishna, and it established the subject as a favorite one for writers. For hundreds of years, a festival has been held in Jayadeva's honor at his birthplace, the small Bengali village of Kenduli. The centerpiece of the celebrations is a performance of the *Gitagovinda*.

Radha and Krishna, from a folio of the Gitagovinda, c. 1550, from Rajasthan.

The sounds of Krishna's flute encouraged the *gopis*, cowgirls, to dance with the renowned lover, shown here playing with the women in a detail from a 19th-century cotton wall-hanging depicting scenes from the life of Krishna.

They looked far and wide until they found Radha slumped on a footpath, alone. She told them how Krishna had led her away from the dance, and they had walked through the forest paths whispering sweet devotions.

She gulped back her tears, and sighed. She said that she had asked Krishna to carry her because she wanted to feel his strong arms lifting her up, and he had at once taken offense. He had gone away from her into the shadows, leaving her slumped on the ground where they had found her.

Then all the women began to call for Krishna, begging him to return and resume their dance. And whether he had gone far away among the trees or was hiding nearby listening, they never knew. But at last, after they had prayed and prayed for his return, they found him back among them. They danced again in the moonlit clearing, and Krishna's magic made it seem to each woman as if he were dancing close to her again.

The rhythm of the steps grew quicker and the intimacy greater, and the girls swooned with delight at Krishna's touch. They could have cried out for joy in the clear night: each woman felt her heart beat against his heart and her breath married to his as she leaned softly along his body.

On and on they danced, for six months, while the night went on without end and the vast moon floated serenely in the sky and the women's ecstasy with Krishna was like a chiming of bells. At the end of that time, all the women bathed with their lover in the sweet waters of the river, still lit by the peaceful moon. Finally they climbed dripping onto the bank and walked back with Krishna to their homes. They slipped softly back inside and found that everything was exactly as it had been when they set out on their amorous adventure—and none of their husbands or family ever knew that they had been away.

The Spirit and the Sword

Krishna plays a key role in the *Mahabharata,* since he is a cousin of both the warring sides, the Pandavas and the Kauravas. The great epic of India, which tells of the conflict between the two groups of royal cousins, probably grew out of hero-songs hailing the feats of Aryan warriors on the plains of northern India around 1000 BCE.

Arjuna's armies attack the Kaurava lines, watched by Brahma and other deities, in this Mughal watercolor, *c.* 1598. The role of the gods in the *Mahabharata* was a complex one since their loyalties were often divided. Some, like Shiva, resolved the dilemma by switching sides before the battle's end.

The *Mahabharata,* the longest epic poem in the world, was written between 300 BCE and 300 CE. The lineage of its heroes starts with the goddess Ganga. In accordance with a deal she had made with the *vasus,* Ganga had killed all her children except the last-born, Bhishma. But she left her husband, Santanu, king of Hastinapur in northern India, and he fell in love with the nymph Satyavati.

To win Satyavati's hand in marriage, Santanu promised her father that their children would inherit his kingdom; Bhishma, the existing heir, agreed to this and promised never to father any children. Before she met the king, the nymph had had a son, Vsaya, after being seduced by a powerful sage, but Vsaya's existence was a secret.

Santanu and Satyavati had two sons, but both died, and the youngest left two young childless wives, Ambika and Ambalika. According to tradition, the closest surviving male was honor-bound to sleep with the wives in order to father an heir. Bhishma refused because he had promised to have no children. The next closest relation was Vsaya, and Satyavati prevailed upon him to do his honorable best. But because no one knew of his existence, Satyavati had to mislead the wives, convincing them that the tall, good-looking Bhishma was in their chamber. When they saw Vsaya, who had the wild eyes and unkempt appearance of an ascetic, they were horrified. Ambalika blanched with fear and her son was called Pandu ("Pale"). Ambika shut her eyes tight and her son, named Dhritarashtra, was born blind.

Pandu inherited the kingdom of Hastinapur and took two wives of his own, Kunti and Madri. Pandu could father no children because he had been cursed by a sage burning with the power of

Demons

In the Mahabharata, the Danavas were said to be both the gods' brothers and their eternal enemies. The gods were caught in a seemingly endless conflict with the forces of evil, who were powered by the boons granted by Brahma.

The demons' boons, won from meditation or practicing austerities, enabled them to come close to matching the gods in power. They were feared as disrupters of ritual, and those who neglected religious rites were often their prey. Agni, the Vedic god of sacrificial fire, became a celebrated slayer of demons.

The most common name for the demons was *asuras*. In the early Vedic period, *asura* meant god. Varuna, who in this era was the chief god, was hailed as "wise Asura" in the *Rig Veda*. But by the later Vedic period, *asuras* signified evil demons and giants.

Other types of dangerous beings included *rakshas* or *rakshakas*, beasts who assumed

A 17th-century mural of marauding demons, from the Lakshmi Narayan temple in Orchha, Madhya Pradesh.

fierce forms as dwarfs, giants and animals. The *nagas* were demon snakes, ruled by Ananta-Shesha (also known as Vasuki). The *pisachas* were frequenters of cemeteries and were believed to feast on decaying flesh.

tapas, but his wife Kunti had been granted a boon by another sage: she could consort with the gods themselves five times. Her first child, Karna, was born after she made love to the sun god Surya. Her second son, Yudhisthira, was fathered by Dharma, god of duty and the law. The next was conceived with the wind god Vayu and was named Bhima. She also bore a warrior son, Arjuna, by the storm god Indra. Her fifth and final chance she passed to her husband's other wife, Madri. She slept with the Ashvins, horsemen of the sun, and gave birth to the twin boys Nakula and Sahadeva.

Karna was to forsake his brothers, so the five boys, Yudhisthira, Bhima, Arjuna, Nakula and Sahadeva, became known as the Pandavas ("Sons of Pandu"). They were set to inherit the throne of Hastinapur, but shortly afterwards their father died, and their blind uncle Dhritarashtra became regent. He had 100 sons of his own, who were known as the Kauravas ("Sons of Kuru") after a king who was an ancestor of both sets of cousins.

Dhritarashtra treated his nephews as members of his own family, and the two groups of cousins grew up alongside each other. The *brahmin* Drona, who had abandoned the life of a priest in order to prove his prowess as a warrior, taught them the arts of war. It soon became clear that the Pandavas—especially the broad-chested Arjuna, son of Indra—were particularly talented.

The Kauravas watched and grew jealous, led in this as in all things by the eldest brother, Duryodhana. One day a practice bout between Duryodhana and Bhima grew so serious that Drona had to haul the scrabbling warriors apart. Another time, Drona, as a test, sent his charges out against his old enemy Draupada, Draupadi's father. Duryodhana and the Kauravas were defeated and sent home, but the Pandavas led by Arjuna captured the king and brought him to Drona. These and other humiliations were too much for Duryodhana. He and his brother Kauravas became sworn enemies of the Pandavas.

Exile and Treachery

The feud between the Kauravas and the Pandavas grew more bitter with every passing year. When Dharma's son, Yudhisthira, came of age and inherited the throne of Hastinapur, the jealous eldest Kaurava, Duryodhana, was ready with a plan to undermine his rule.

Duryodhana was his father's eldest and favorite son. It was easy for him to persuade his father, Dhritarashtra, to refuse the throne to the eldest Pandava and instead give it to him. He even won Dhritarashtra's approval for a murder plot to do away with the Pandavas once and for all.

He invited his cousins to a celebration at a remote house set deep in the countryside. But he had his servants baste the walls of the house with butter, for he had issued orders that the house be burned down, to kill the Pandavas and make their deaths look like a terrible accident. Before they went to the house, the Pandavas were warned of the plot. They fled with their mother Kunti to a distant forest; the house burned down and Duryodhana believed his cousins had been killed.

The Pandavas disguised themselves as wandering *brahmins* and had many adventures. In the course of one, Arjuna won an archery contest whose prize was the hand of the beautiful princess Draupadi. But when he returned to his mother and told her that he had won a fine prize, she—not realizing what it was—told him to share it with his brothers. He had to follow her wishes, and she could not go back on what she had said, so the five brothers shared Draupadi.

In the course of the archery contest, however, Arjuna had been recognized despite his disguise, and the news travelled fast to the Kauravas that their cousins were still alive. The Kauravas could not agree how best to do away with their great rivals. In the end, however, the *brahmin* Drona persuaded his brothers to invite the Pandavas home and offer them half the kingdom.

The Pandavas returned to the Hastinapur region and took over a desert area named Khandavaprastha. They built a splendid new city named Indraprastha (near modern Delhi) and invited the Kauravas to see it and to attend a consecration ceremony. The consecration was so splendid, and the sacrifices so grand, that Duryodhana felt sick with envy and left more determined than ever to bring his cousins low.

The Kauravas' first act of reprisal was to build a new hall filled with crystal glass and adorned with lapis lazuli and gold. It had 1,000 columns

The Kauravas became highly devious in their attempts to humiliate their cousins, the Pandavas, who epitomized just principles and righteous action. This watercolor, from the Punjab Hills and dating from the middle of the 18th century, shows the fateful game of dice in which the unwary Yudhisthira lost everything he owned to Duryodhana, including the Pandavas' kingdom and his innocent wife, Draupadi, who can be seen in the adjoining chamber.

the end of the game, he had bet and lost his own personal possessions, the Pandavas' kingdom, their freedom and even his beloved wife Draupadi.

Duryodhana drained his cup and laughed openly. Then he sent his brother Dushashana to fetch Draupadi from an adjoining chamber. Dushashana dragged her in by her hair, taunting her that she was now his slave girl and he could do what he wished with her. In front of the roomful of jeering, laughing Kauravas he began to tear at her clothes. But Draupadi prayed chastely to Vishnu to save her modesty, and the god protected her. Each layer of clothing that Dushashana tore off was instantly replaced by another.

Duryodhana was maddened by his triumph and pulled Draupadi into his lap, scrabbling at her clothes. Bhima burnt with righteous fury and pledged that he would kill Dushashana and drink his blood and then smash Duryodhana's thigh in revenge for this indecency.

At that moment, King Dhritarashtra heard a bloodcurdling jackal's howl, and he knew with awful certainty that it prefigured the downfall of the Kauravas. He spoke kind words to Draupadi, offering her three boons as a small recompense for her mistreatment. For the first two, the princess asked for her own freedom and for that of her five husbands. Then she spoke proudly to her tormentors, saying that in order to thrive in the world, her husbands only needed liberty—and she contemptuously rejected the third boon.

Duryodhana managed to persuade his father to allow one more throw of the dice. He said that the animosity between the two sets of cousins was now so intense that the only way to avoid violence was for them to part. Whoever lost the dice game, he said, should go into forest exile for thirteen years. The two sides agreed. The Pandavas lost. Wearily disguising themselves as wandering beggars, they set off for a forest hermitage.

But outside the city, Arjuna separated from his brothers. A sage had told him to travel to the mighty Himalayas and seek the help of the gods, and so he told his brothers he would meet up with them later on in their travels. He found the god

and 100 doors and was just as splendid as the Pandavas' palace. Duryodhana invited his cousins to an opening party at which he approached Yudhisthira and challenged him to a dice-throwing session. But it was all carefully planned—for he had devised a plot with his devious uncle Shakuni, who knew all the tricks there were for enticing an opponent into rash bets.

Yudhisthira accepted the challenge although he was not a gambler. They began with small sums of money and jewels, but the betting escalated—and all the time Yudhisthira lost steadily until, by

81

Shiva and managed to obtain his favor. Shiva gave the great warrior the *pasupata*, a heavenly weapon, and other gods also gave Arjuna arms. Then he met his father Indra, who welcomed him into Swarga, his heaven. Arjuna stayed there for many months preparing for battle. Finally he returned to Earth in a vehicle driven by Indra's charioteer, Matali, and met up with his brothers.

During their exile, the brothers performed many great feats. In the last year of their exile, the Pandavas travelled in disguise to help the king of Virata, who had been attacked by the voracious Kaurava armies. Arjuna single-handedly defeated an entire Kaurava detachment, and in gratitude the king of Virata offered to help the Pandavas regain their kingdom of Hastinapur. So fate moved a full-scale conflict between the two sides ever nearer.

Both sides turned to Krishna, who was a cousin to both the Pandavas and the Kauravas. He said he would join one side as an adviser and provide a vast army for the other. Arjuna had first choice and opted to have Krishna's counsel.

Later the Pandavas sent Krishna to speak to Duryodhana in an attempt to avert the conflict. But Duryodhana had his heart set on bloodshed, and he refused to negotiate. While in the Kauravas' court, Krishna took care to speak to Karna, suggesting that he switch sides in the war. Karna refused but promised not to kill any of his brothers in the heat of the battle.

The scene was set for conflict. The two vast armies drew up on the plain of Kurukshetra, prepared to follow their duty as warriors and fight to the death to defend the honor of their family.

A Fateful Game of Dice

Nala, husband of the divinely beautiful Damayanti, gambled away his wealth and his kingdom just as Yudhisthira had done. As a result, Nala, too, almost lost his beautiful bride.

One day Nala, handsome ruler of Nishadha, caught a wondrous speaking swan whose strong wings were dusted with gold. The bird offered to fly to Damayanti, the beautiful princess of neighboring Vidarbha, and praise the prince to her. In this way, the couple fell in love before they ever met.

Shortly afterwards, Damayanti held a ceremony to pick a husband and chose Nala. The pair lived together in great happiness for twelve years and had two beautiful children. But one day Nala made a small error in his purification rituals. Kali swept into his body and drove Nala to challenge his brother Pushkara to a game of dice in which Nala lost everything but his wife. He left the city, but Damayanti followed him.

They wandered in the forests, until Nala—still driven by Kali's evil urgings—abandoned Damayanti while she slept. When she woke, she wandered far and wide, looking for him in vain. Eventually, she was given refuge in a palace at Chedi.

Nala, meanwhile, had rescued the serpent Karkotaka from a sage's curse. In return the snake bit him, transforming him into the dwarf Vahuka and causing Kali enough pain to drive out the wicked deity. As Vahuka, Nala became chariot driver for Rituparna, king of Ayodhya.

Some time later, Damayanti was recognized by a wandering priest and returned to live with her father. Then Bhima sent priests out to look for Nala with a message from Damayanti, begging him to return. One of them became suspicious when he met Vahuka, so Damayanti held another ceremony inviting Rituparna so Vahuka would come too. When, at the feast, she called Vahuka to her, he

confessed his true identity. He
became once more the handsome
Nala and the loving couple were
reunited. Before they parted,
Rituparna instructed Nala in dice-
playing. Nala then challenged his
brother to another game of dice
and defeated him. He had it in his
power to destroy the man who had
brought him so much misery, but
he forgave him and allowed him
to live at peace in his kingdom.

**The impulsive Nala falls in love with
Damayanti as the swan describes her
legendary beauty, which had enchanted
many, including several of the gods.**

The Song of the Lord

Leading Pandava warrior Arjuna paused before battle, filled with doubts. Krishna, his princely charioteer, eased his worries by advising him on what he should do in the conflict. Then, to Arjuna's great astonishment, he revealed the divine reality within him.

The Kauravas faced the Pandavas on the sweeping Kurukshetra plain. Duryodhana spoke in ringing tones to the massed Kaurava troops, and they roared approval and blew on their conch horns. The Pandavas responded at once, and the sound of their horns and martial shouts seemed to shake the whole of heaven and Earth. But Arjuna asked his charioteer, Prince Krishna, to drive forward into the land between the armies so he could have a last look at the two sides of his tragically divided family before the onset of the battle.

On the eve of battle, Krishna counsels Arjuna on the immortality of the soul. From a 19th-century manuscript of the *Bhagavad Gita*.

Krishna expounded to him on his duty. He told Arjuna that he had no cause to be sorrowful: the souls of all those gathered on the battlefield were immortal, and he could not slay the living core of any soldier. In that sense, death and bloodshed were no more than an illusion. As a warrior, it was Arjuna's *dharma*—his proper and essential quality—to fight and be brave. He should perform his duty, but with a sense of detachment from personal reward. He must go resolutely into battle.

The charioteer went on to teach Arjuna more about the divine core that exists in all humans and also lies beneath all the manifestations of the universe. He taught the prince that the individual can escape delusions by devotion to a personal god.

Arjuna was reminded that his essential or divine self—the *atman*—would never taste death. While human life ended in death, it was followed by rebirth, when the soul assumed a new body. To experience the reality of the *atman*, he said, Arjuna must detach himself from selfish desires.

In the course of their talk, Arjuna had a vision of Krishna as the lord of all. He appeared as bright as 1,000 suns, not only the support of the universe but also its body, draped in heavenly garments and sweet flowers, infinite in all directions with countless arms, legs, mouths and colors. Seeing Krishna-Vishnu finally as a burning destroyer, Arjuna was terrified and asked his friend to forgive him if he had ever treated him disrespectfully and failed to recognize his true majesty. Then Krishna reverted to a more bearable human form. Subsequently, Arjuna worshipped Krishna, who declared to him that the goal of the individual soul was union with Vishnu—realization of the union between *atman* and *brahman*—which would bring escape from the cycle of death and rebirth.

The narrative of the great conflict is put on hold for the course of this discussion, which is contained in a separate book known as the *Bhagavad Gita* ("Song of the Lord"), added to the *Mahabharata* sometime before 400 CE.

Some scholars see the discussion between Krishna and Arjuna as a kind of bridging passage to the main part of the *Bhagavad Gita*, which is a revelation of the human relationship to the divine. Others see the entire *Mahabharata* as an allegory of the struggle between good and evil. From this perspective, Arjuna is a religious seeker receiving instruction on the path to enlightenment. The *Bhagavad Gita* has also been interpreted as representing a religious debate between two sides of an individual, with Arjuna as the human personality and Krishna the *atman,* or divine self.

The *Bhagavad Gita* is in parts a Vaishnavite document, for in revealing himself as the Supreme Soul, the divine reality, Krishna is an aspect of Vishnu. The impersonal reality, *brahman*, once identified with Brahma, is now identified with Vishnu and given a personal face. The poem is certainly the work of more than one author and adopts different and essentially incompatible religious perspectives. In the *Bhagavad Gita* the divine is a personal god; an object of devotion; the impersonal supreme soul, or *brahman*; and the immortal self within each individual. The *Gita* is endlessly interpreted because it is so rich and various. Some Hindus see Krishna's speeches as the word of God revealed.

Warfare forms a constant background to Hindu myth and history. After the Aryan invasion of 1500 BCE, India endured millennia of dynastic struggles until the coming of the Mughals in the 16th century. These Muslim emperors, whose pride in warfare is suggested by this 17th-century helmet, ruled until the British came and exploited their decline in the 1700s.

85

Eighteen Days at Kurukshetra

The insulting behavior of Duryodhana and his Kaurava brothers came back to haunt them during their epic battle with the Pandavas at Kurukshetra. Warriors gave their all as the conflict swept back and forth for eighteen days before coming to its dreadful conclusion.

Despite his age, Bhishma, commander of the Kaurava army, carried the battle to the Pandavas. As son of the goddess Ganga, he found no equal on the battlefield. But Bhishma knew that he would die at the hands of Shikhandin, one of the Pandavas' brothers-in-law, whom he had grievously insulted in a previous incarnation. And when Shikhandin stepped forward with Arjuna, the mighty general Bhishma was slain.

The *brahmin* Drona then took up the Kaurava cause, and at once dispatched Draupada, his oldest enemy (see page 79). But Drona, too, was soon slain by the cunning Pandavas. So Karna, son of Surya, the eldest of the Pandavas, came forward and sought out Arjuna. They became locked in fierce combat, both wielding weapons of the gods. Arjuna used those given to him by Shiva when he had visited the Himalayas at the start of his exile from Hastinapur. Karna had a javelin that Indra had given him. The two fought long and hard as equals until Karna unleashed the power of his javelin. When it missed his foe, he knew that he was doomed and, cowering in the shadow of Arjuna's chariot, he begged for mercy. The Pandava general only laughed. Honor, he scoffed, had meant nothing to Karna on the day that Draupadi was insulted. He killed Karna, and the sky over the battlefield grew black as Surya mourned the death of his son.

The Battle of Kurukshetra, the dramatic climax of the *Mahabharata*, captured the imagination of generations of Indian artists. This cotton wall-hanging, showing the battle at its height, was executed for the Rajah of Chamba in the 18th century.

The tide of battle turned decisively against the Kauravas. One by one they fell, and revenge was sweet for the Pandavas. The cheating dice-player Shakuni wept and begged for his life before he was killed by Sahadeva, the youngest Pandava. Dushashana, who had torn Draupadi's clothes in his lustful desire to see her naked, died at the hand of Bhima. The victorious warrior swelled with triumph as he fulfilled his threat (see page 81) by drinking Dushashana's lifeblood.

As dawn rose over the bloodstained battlefield, there were only a handful of Kauravas alive, and the air was thick with vultures. Duryodhana was hiding in a lake, but Yudhisthira tracked him there. Duryodhana was by now a broken man. He sobbed and offered Yudhisthira the entire Kaurava kingdom. But Yudhisthira insisted on fighting. Finally Duryodhana emerged and agreed to individual combat with each Pandava. Forward stepped Bhima, who struck him down and then watched him crawl back to his own lines.

The battle had been won. But Drona's son, Ashvatthaman, was still thirsty for revenge. He crept into the Pandava camp where in the shadows he encountered the terrifying form of Shiva. Ashvatthaman fell down in awe, but the great god declared he could no longer protect the Pandavas and swept into the soldier's body. The killer went on his way, and everyone he encountered that night in the Pandava camp was slaughtered. Dhrishadyumna, brother-in-law of Draupadi, and her five sons were among the victims, but the Pandavas themselves were not there, since they were looting the Kaurava camp.

At first light Ashvatthaman raced across the battlefield and woke Duryodhana to show him the heads he had taken, for he thought they were the Pandavas themselves. Duryodhana felt a welcome wave of triumph, but then he looked more closely and saw that these were not his enemies' heads. Duryodhana's joy soured and turned to bile. He fell down in bitterness and died.

After so much bloodshed, peace did eventually settle on this troubled family and across the bloodstained land. The Pandavas reached an agreement with their blind uncle Dhritarashtra. Finally, Yudhisthira acceded to the throne of Hastinapur—as he should have done years earlier. He was a good king, under whom people prospered and enjoyed the fruits of plenty.

The Journey to Paradise

As the glory of their victory over the Kauravas faded into the past, the Pandavas decided to leave war and politics behind. They journeyed to the mighty Himalayas, home of the gods, and there intended to prepare for death.

When the victorious Pandavas returned to Hastinapur, they did not forget that many of their kinsmen had died. As the new king, Yudhisthira performed a horse sacrifice to express his earthly glory, but he also wanted to make an act of penance for his sins. When the stallion returned from its year's wanderings, a great celebration was held. Princes, and even gods, including Krishna and Indra, came to honor the Pandavas.

A late 16th- or early 17th-century bronze statue of a horse. While horse sacrifices, such as the one performed by Yudhisthira, are a recurrent feature of the *Puranas*, the animals themselves were not common in India until the coming of the Mughals.

Some time after this, the Pandavas declared their intention of leaving Hastinapur in order to prepare for death. With their wife Draupadi and a single faithful hound, the five brothers set out for the Himalayas in the simple, ragged clothes of pilgrims. Their goal was the mythical Mount Meru, where, they believed, they would find Indra ruling his blissful heaven, Swarga.

On the way, Draupadi, Sahadeva, Nakula, Arjuna and Bhima all died, leaving Yudhisthira and the hound to ascend the Himalayan foothills. Finally, the blue skies opened to reveal the sacred Mount Meru, and Yudhisthira soon found his way to Swarga's towering gates.

Indra, spine of the world and master of the clouds, came to greet the hero. When the great god said that dogs could not be admitted to heaven, the animal disappeared, and Yudhisthira saw his own father, Dharma, god of duty, standing beside him. They embraced happily and entered Swarga. But then Yudhisthira saw his enemy Duryodhana seated on a throne, and he knew he could not stay. Instead, he found his way to the place of punishment where, among the screams of the tortured, he heard the voices of Draupadi, Arjuna and his brothers. He decided to stay there and help them in their pain, but in that instant, the scene disappeared. It had been an illusion.

He found himself back on Earth. As an aged solitary pilgrim, he made his way to the sacred Ganges, and when he had bathed in its life-giving waters, his soul burst from his tired body and flew to Swarga. He met Krishna, Draupadi and the other Pandavas; he also met the virtuous souls among his enemies such as Bhishma and Drona. There, beyond time, he consorted with his glorious kinsmen in the presence of the gods.

A Final Wish

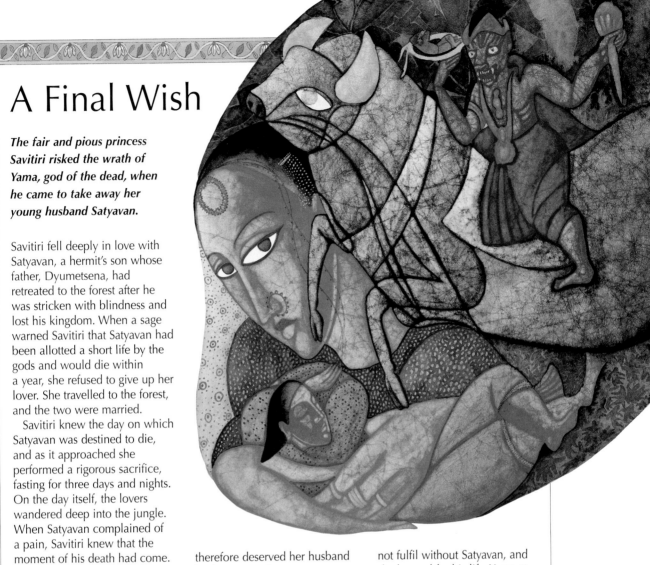

The fair and pious princess Savitiri risked the wrath of Yama, god of the dead, when he came to take away her young husband Satyavan.

Savitiri fell deeply in love with Satyavan, a hermit's son whose father, Dyumetsena, had retreated to the forest after he was stricken with blindness and lost his kingdom. When a sage warned Savitiri that Satyavan had been allotted a short life by the gods and would die within a year, she refused to give up her lover. She travelled to the forest, and the two were married.

Savitiri knew the day on which Satyavan was destined to die, and as it approached she performed a rigorous sacrifice, fasting for three days and nights. On the day itself, the lovers wandered deep into the jungle. When Satyavan complained of a pain, Savitiri knew that the moment of his death had come. She persuaded him to lie down and close his eyes, while she cushioned his head in her lap. Red-eyed Yama appeared in a blood-red cloak and with a glittering crown. He took Satyavan's soul from his body and bound it with the noose he always kept for the dead.

Yama stalked away, but Savitiri went after him. He told her to go back but she refused, telling him that she had been a perfect and loyal wife, had performed many powerful sacrifices and that she therefore deserved her husband back. Her persistence was so great that Yama offered her four wishes—anything except Satyavan's life. Savitiri asked for her father-in-law to have both his eyesight and his kingdom restored. Then she asked for her father and herself to be given 100 sons. Yama agreed and then sent her on her way. Yet still she refused to go. Impressed with her devotion, the god then granted her one final boon. Savitiri said he had granted her a wish, 100 sons, that she could not fulfil without Satyavan, and she begged for his life. Yama at once released Satyavan's soul and Savitiri found herself back in the forest, with her husband's head still cradled on her lap. He woke, and they walked gently back to the hermitage. And in the years that followed, all her wishes were granted.

Savitiri, aware that Satyavan's death is near, cradles his head, and waits as Yama, the flame-haired lord of death, arrives to take away his soul.

A YEAR OF FESTIVALS

India's manifold divinities are feted in a bewildering array of festivals held all over the country throughout the year. Some, such as Diwali, the great festival of light, are national events, held annually. Others are occasional. The Kumbha Mela takes place only every three years with its most significant observance at Allahabad every twelfth. Most, however, are local affairs, celebrating a single god or goddess, or commemorating a significant event, like Tarnetar Fair in Gujarat, which honors the marriage of Arjuna with Draupadi in the *Mahabharata*. The festivals are extensions of private worship, giving life to sacred images and spreading their influence throughout a region. They aim to purify, renew or dispel demonic forces. Their date is determined by the cycle of the moon, so their point in the calendar varies from year to year. By reflecting the cycles of life, they bind communities together and encourage propitious relations with the gods.

Right: Krishna and his female companions celebrate the festival of Holi, in a Guler watercolor from Himachal Pradesh, *c.* 1780. This festival, during which many roles are reversed including those of caste and sex, is celebrated with a passion and energy typical of India's religious events. A means of worshipping and animating various deities, the elaborate rituals, played out at festival times, are an integral part of Hinduism.

JAN/FEB: BENESHWAR FAIR
Bhil tribespeople gather in Rajasthan
to bathe in the Som and Mahi rivers,
committing the ashes of dead relatives
to the water and cleansing themselves.
They then worship images of Shiva.

FEB/MAR: HOLI FESTIVAL
This festival celebrates the mischievous
Lord Krishna and is one of the liveliest in
India. Huge crowds assemble to sing,
dance and, most famously, hurl colored
dyes in the air and at each other.

APRIL: KUMBHA MELA
Every three years Kumbha Mela
celebrates the triumph of good over evil
through noble ideas. The greatest event
is at Allahabad every twelfth year, when
Sadhus gather to take a ritual bath.

APRIL/MAY: POORAM
People meet to celebrate Pooram, the
Kerala temple festival, on Kovalam beach.
At twilight, elephants carry images of
Shiva through the crowds. Fireworks light
the sky until dawn.

AUG/SEPT: GANESHA CHATURI
Around Bombay, crafted images of
Ganesha, the god of good fortune, are
carried in the streets and adorned with
offerings. Then, amid the sound of drums
and cymbals, he is offered up to the sea.

SEPT/OCT: DURGA PUJA
This ten-day festival, held in west Bengal
and other parts of eastern India, focuses
on Devi, the demon-slaying goddess.
At the climax of the festival, an image
of Durga is submerged in a nearby river.

SEPT/OCT: RAMLILA
Dussehra is one of the most important
national festivals, but it varies in style
and content from place to place. In
Varanasi, it is celebrated with a ten-day
performance of the epic *Ramayana*.

OCT/NOV: PUSHKAR MELA
This festival, which is accompanied by
a camel fair, centers on the temple of
Brahma, near Pushkar Lake in Rajasthan.
For four days, until the moon is full,
people trade camels and worship.

OCT/NOV: CHHAT PUJA
Devotees propitiate the sun god Surya by
performing arduous rituals in exchange
for good fortune. Food and other gifts are
then offered to the nearest source of
water, preferably the holy Ganges River.

MOTHERS OF CREATION

When the 1,000-headed demon Andhaka ("Darkness") invaded Indra's heaven, Brahma, Vishnu and Shiva met to discuss how to retaliate. Each followed his own powerful thoughts, and then they all happened to look at each other. A brilliant light appeared where the gods' gazes met and coalesced into a woman of captivating beauty. All three gods wanted to possess her, so they agreed to divide her into three—a white goddess who took the name Sarasvati and became Brahma's wife; a red one named Lakshmi who married Vishnu; and a black one, Parvati, who became Shiva's consort. The black goddess had terrible powers that would be more than a match for Andhaka.

There are countless myths of the creation of this primal goddess. In some, she exists before the gods themselves; in others, she is a vital force that emerges from them. Durga, for example, manifests as a female warrior to save the gods from a demon made mighty by the power of a boon.

All the goddesses are considered aspects of one great female deity. Through the period of the epics (300 years on either side of the birth of Christ) and of the *Puranas* (the medieval era) the idea developed that each god derived his power from the goddess he had been given as a consort. Sarasvati was the creative energy of Brahma, and Lakshmi was part of Vishnu's role as protector and preserver. The idea was particularly applied to Shiva, whose wife was variously known as Sati, Parvati, Durga, Kali and Uma. Often god and goddess were considered to be eternally linked aspects of *brahman*. When Durga-Kali danced on the body of Shiva, it was an image of his union with Shakti, the Mother Goddess, showing that the god was essentially inactive, dead for all purposes, without his complementary female energy. This idea was reflected in the symbol of the male *lingam* encircled by the female *yoni*, and by the androgynous god-goddess Ardhanarisvara.

In modern times the worship of Shakti has become as important as the cults of Vishnu and Shiva. For devotees of the Mother Goddess, Shakti is the active, manifesting aspect of *brahman*. According to one interpretation, the universe comes into being through Shakti. She is the mother of everything. At the end of each age, or *yuga*, it is Shakti who withdraws the manifested universe back into her being, and in the dark night between creations, all that exists lies at rest in her.

Opposite: **Parvati was in love with Shiva but won him only after meditating in the mountains for seven long years. This ivory relief from south India, *c.* 1766, celebrates their eventual marriage.**

Below: **Shiva's face adorns this *lingam,* set within a *yoni.* Their union symbolizes how Shakti and Shiva, female and male, are eternally linked. From Vrindaban, *c.* 18th century.**

Forces of War and Fertility

Archaeological finds at places such as Mohenjo-Daro in the Indus Valley suggest that people there worshipped fertility goddesses nearly 5,000 years ago. Although belief in a supreme female divinity fell away after the Aryan invasion, faith in goddesses of war or fertility later reemerged to become a major factor in Hinduism.

The faith of the Aryans centered on a cluster of male divinities. In the *Vedas*, goddesses were essentially subordinate to gods and were viewed as their consorts. The goddesses were generally personifications of natural features and forces or related to objects associated with ritual worship. Ida was the goddess of food offerings; Vac, the goddess of speech. Sarasvati, later wife of Brahma, began life as a Vedic river goddess alongside Ganga and Yamuna (see box opposite). The ever-youthful Usas was a personification of the dawn and was widely popular; there are several entrancing hymns in her honor in the *Rig Veda*.

But one of the goddesses, Aditi, was in some sense a Vedic version of the all-encompassing Great Goddess. Aditi represented infinity as the upholder of the Earth and sky. She was benevolent and associated with light. She was also linked to

Aspects of the goddess encompass two clear opposites: the gentle mother of procreation and beauty, and the murderous avenger. Here Kali, an example of the latter tendency, beheads a man, in this watercolor from Bundi, *c.* 1650.

the cow—for she was the source of life in the universe as a cow is a source of nourishing milk. Aditi's sons, the Adityas, included Varuna and were often said to be twelve in number, representing the months of the year. However, in the original myth of the Adityas, there were eight, seven of whom the goddess loved while the eighth she threw away. The divine smith Tvastr took the eighth child and made him into Vivasvat, the rising sun. The parts he did not use tumbled to Earth and came to life as elephants who, because of their origins, had a divine element within them. Aditi's role later expanded to make her mother of all the gods.

A Temperamental Muse

Brahma's wife Sarasvati is the embodiment of his power, the instrument of creation and the energy that drives his actions. She is revered as the goddess of the creative arts and particularly of the sacred pursuits of poetry and music.

Sarasvati is identified with the Vedic goddess of speech, Vac. She is the source of the holy scriptures and is said to have created Sanskrit, the ancient and sacred language of the Hindus. The holy *Vedas* may have emerged from Brahma's head, but it was her energy that formed them.

From the earliest times, Sarasvati has been goddess of the Sarasvati River, a once westward-flowing stream that emerged from the Himalayas in northern India. Now dried up, the river retains a symbolic presence and is said to run underground and flow invisibly into the mighty Ganges.

Scholars believe that Sarasvati's link with riverside hymn-making and religious ritual led to her identification with Vac. It was Vac who was originally named "Mother of the *Vedas*" and this epithet passed to Sarasvati. Viraj, the female energy that is part of Purusha in some versions of his myth (see pages 28–29), is also identified with Sarasvati.

The goddess was renowned for her quarrelsome nature. According to one story, Vishnu once had three wives—Sarasvati, Lakshmi and Ganga—but the trio argued so much among themselves that Vishnu grew weary and decided to offer two of them to his fellow gods. He gave Ganga to Shiva and Sarasvati to Brahma. But Sarasvati was soon responsible for Brahma's lack of devotees: one day Brahma summoned his new companion to attend an important religious sacrifice, but she told him to wait because she was not yet ready for it. In his fury he married Gayatri, a sage's daughter, and when Sarasvati found out, she cursed Brahma to enjoy just one day of worship each year.

This 12th-century marble statue from Pallu in Rajasthan shows Sarasvati as goddess of learning. She is usually white-skinned and is sometimes shown riding a swan or peacock, or standing on a lotus flower. She is often depicted with a lyre.

A Widow's Sacrifice

Sati made the ultimate act of self-sacrifice in burning herself to prove her husband Shiva's worth. Her name was forever linked with widows who made a similar gesture of devotion when their husbands died.

At one time, in certain communities in India, a living widow would be burned on her husband's funeral pyre. Some cases may have been voluntary, but most were enforced by custom.

The Sanskrit noun *sati*—derived from *sat*, meaning true or good—was applied to the cremated wives, and European missionaries later gave the name to the act itself. The British anglicized the word as "suttee."

Scholars do not know when the practice began. In the Vedic era it was only symbolic—the wife lay down on the pyre with her husband before it was lit and was then helped away by mourners. *Sati* was most evident among the *brahmin* class from the late-seventeenth century in Bengal, and it was given added momentum by a legal code that allowed widows to inherit property. The practice was banned in British India in 1829, but it continued in some Indian states until the middle of the nineteenth century.

A ritual that began as a purely symbolic gesture eventually saw wives consumed in the flames of their husband's funeral pyre. This watercolor of a *sati* ceremony is from Tanjore, southern India, c. 1800.

By the fifth century CE, the worship of the Great Goddess was playing a significant part in Hinduism. This revived religious impulse combined the ancient fertility cults with the personified goddesses of the Aryan pantheon. Shakti now took many forms. Devi, derived from Sanskrit *div* ("to shine"), was a generic name that encompassed them all under the feminine form of *deva*, god.

At various times Devi is known as Parvati, Lakshmi, Uma, Durga, Kali and many other names. The goddess could be benevolent like Parvati, or fiercely malevolent like Durga and Kali. But even in her fierce forms she is said to continue to nourish her devotees. Many local and tribal deities were assimilated in the goddess. Village goddesses still widely worshipped today are understood to be aspects of her (see page 112).

Shiva's First Wife

From around the seventh century CE, Devi was often portrayed as the wife of Shiva. The god first married her in the form of Sati, daughter of Brahma's son Daksha. Sati was a devotee of Shiva, but Daksha disapproved of the god because of his unkempt appearance. So when Daksha held a *swayamvara* ceremony to choose a husband for his daughter, he invited all the gods save Shiva. But Sati would marry no one else, so she focused all her energy on him, and when she flung her garland in the air, the god himself suddenly appeared to catch it and claim her as his wife.

The feud between Daksha and Shiva worsened. Eventually, at a sacrificial ceremony, Sati decided to prove her husband's great worth to everyone present. She hurled herself into the fire pit and gave her body up to the flames.

Far away, Shiva knew at once what had happened, and he stormed into the sacrifice, driving the other gods before him and striking off Daksha's head in his fury. Then he tenderly picked up Sati's body and began a sad dance through the world, spreading suffering as he went. Vishnu followed, and to ease Shiva's pain he cut away at Sati's body as Shiva danced. It fell to Earth in fifty-one pieces and, wherever a part of Sati landed, a holy site was set up by Shakti's devotees.

The temple at Kamakhya in Assam marks the spot where Sati's *yoni* is said to have fallen. One of her toes supposedly landed near the Ganges and is marked by the Kalighat temple. The place became known as Kaliksetra ("Place of Kali") and in its anglicized form is called Calcutta.

Devi next returned to Shiva as the moody but beautiful Parvati. Another benevolent form of the goddess was golden-skinned Uma, with whom Shiva is often shown enjoying domestic bliss.

Principal among the malevolent forms were Durga and Kali. Many-armed Durga was a terrifying slayer of demons and she was often honored with sacrifices. Goats and other animals were sacrificed to her each autumn at a festival in Calcutta. Until the middle of the nineteenth century, human sacrifices were also part of her cult.

Kali was often said to have sprung from the forehead of Durga. She first appeared in the Hindu pantheon as a form of Devi in around 500 CE in the *Markandeya Purana*, her black body horribly thin, a necklace of fifty human skulls around her neck. Like Shiva in his Bhairava form, Kali frequented graveyards and cremation grounds. Sometimes she was Bhairavi, a feminine aspect of Bhairava.

Karni-Mata, shown here on a brass temple door from Bikaner in Rajasthan, was an incarnation of Durga. The 14th-century shrine was dedicated to the worship of rats, which are believed to be the souls of Mata devotees and carry Durga on visits to Earth.

Durga and the Buffalo Demon

The Great Goddess took the form of the fierce warrior Durga in order to defend her fellow deities against the demons. Their leader Mahishasura—a fierce buffalo with a man's head— had vast powers derived from his mother's austerities. At the head of a monstrous army, he seized the celestial realm from the gods, driving them in every direction.

After Mahishasura, the hideous buffalo demon, had smashed the armies of the gods and sent them helpless into the wilderness seeking refuge, the desperate deities went to Brahma and begged for help. The giver of boons listened attentively to their complaints and then took them to seek the advice of Vishnu and Shiva.

As all the gods in conference bemoaned Mahishasura's wickedness, righteous anger swelled within them until they could contain it no longer. Rage flowed from them in the form of pure fire, and the flames mingled in a vast ball like a celestial mountain. A goddess, fully formed and beautiful in her ferocity, emerged from the raging flames. She was filled with the force of the gods, which gave her awesome power. Her head burned with Shiva's potency, and her arms were filled with the mightiness of Vishnu, while Brahma's energy took the form of her feet. Other parts of her body were derived from lesser gods and celestial bodies—her hair from Yama, her breasts from the moon, her thighs from Varuna and her toes from the sun. With so much divine energy concentrated in her, she was more powerful than any individual deity and could vanquish any demon.

In some versions of the myth, the goddess had appeared long before as the *shakti,* or creative energy, of Shiva.

The gods ran to her when they were thrown out of heaven by the buffalo demon, and they lent her their weapons for the battle. She took those commonly associated with each god—the discus of Vishnu, the trident of Shiva and the thunderbolt of Indra. Images of many-armed Durga show her holding a divine weapon in each of her hands.

Blazing with power, Durga mounted her charger, the deep-voiced lion, and went forth to fight the gods' enemy. Mahishasura took the form of a warrior and appeared with vast battalions of demon soldiers at his back, but Durga possessed enough power within her to defeat the entire host, which soon fled, seized with terror.

Mahishasura swelled with fury when he saw her overcome his army. He reverted to his buffalo form and charged at the goddess's troops, trampling on some and scoring others with his horns. The demon was in a frenzy of rage. His great tail swept through the ocean, causing tidal waves that destroyed whole islands; with his two vast horns, he unearthed the roots of the tallest mountains and sent the peaks flying through the air; clouds in the sky were torn to shreds by his crazed bucking and leaping.

All this time Durga watched calmly, but when Mahishasura attacked her lion, she could contain herself no longer. She took a rope and with a single swing lassoed the buffalo, tying him up in an instant. Mahishasura then transformed himself into a lion. Durga cut off his head with a decisive blow, but the evil creature at once became a warrior armed with sword and shield. Durga swiftly seized her bow and shot him with arrows, but the man turned into a trumpeting elephant, which attacked her lion charger with its powerful trunk. Durga then sliced off the trunk with her sword.

A serene Durga, riding on a lion, prepares for combat with Mahishasura, in a watercolor from Rajasthan, *c.* 1750. The warlike goddess was called upon to help the gods, who were powerless against the demon.

99

The conquest of demons by the Great Goddess is a recurrent theme in Hindu art and mythology. Here, Devi is victorious once again, in a 13th-century sculpture from Mysore. The goddess took the name Durga after slaying a demon of this name.

By now the demon had exhausted his disguises, and he reverted to his familiar buffalo form. But his rage was stronger than ever. His roars resounded through the air, and the entire universe shook as he snorted and pawed the ground, hurling great mountain rocks at Durga. The goddess knocked his missiles from the sky with her well-aimed arrows. Then she drank the wine of sacrifice, rich with the blood of sacrificial victims. Again and again she drained the cup, all the while laughing at the demon, who pranced before her deranged by anger. Full of sacrificial wine, the Great Goddess flung herself on his back and delivered a devastating kick to his neck. So great was her power that the blow caused the buffalo to retch and so expel Mahishasura's demon form. As he was ejected like bile from the buffalo's mouth, the goddess seized him by the hair and sliced his head off.

Mahishasura fell down dead at Durga's feet. A great clamor filled the universe as all women and men, all creatures and all gods hailed her victory over evil. The gods came quickly to praise Durga with sweet flowers and delicate incense, and the heavenly nymphs danced for her pleasure.

On another occasion, two demons, Sumbha and Nisumbha, had performed long austerities and become invulnerable to any god. Now they were free to run wild. Durga agreed to assist the helpless gods and descended to the Himalayas as a beautiful maiden with shining hair and lotus eyes.

Two travelling demons, Vanda and Munda, spotted her there and told their master, Sumbha, of the woman they had seen on a Himalayan mountainside playing with a lion. Sumbha was filled with lust and sent a servant to bring her to his palace.

But the goddess said that she would only marry the man who could subdue her in one-to-one combat. The servant tried to convince her that Sumbha was a great warrior and not to be trifled with, but Durga was not impressed. Back the messenger

Demonic activity was always seen in terms of a spiritual or physical chaos that subverted the natural order of the gods. Here, fields of the Gangetic plains lie flooded by a monsoon, which has wreaked the kind of havoc caused by the demon Durga before he was slain by Devi.

travelled, bearing the disappointing news for Sumbha. The demon king flew into a rage, and in his anger he sent a vast army to capture the maiden and drag her back to his palace.

The demons arrived and gave her one last chance to change her mind. But faced with these troops, the goddess grew hot with anger. From her forehead erupted the terrible goddess Kali, her face the deepest black, emaciated as if starved of grain and flesh. She opened her mouth, and the universe resounded with her roar. With a laugh she devoured the entire demon army, stuffing warriors and their elephants together into her mouth. Kali then beheaded Vanda and Munda and presented their heads to Durga.

Another demon army, this time led by Sumbha himself, arrived on the Himalayan slopes. Issuing from Kali's mouth, the sacred syllable "Om" shook the universe, and the *shakti* of the gods came forth from Durga's body to join the battle. The demons fled in fear, while Kali simply laughed. Then Durga reabsorbed the *shakti* and went into battle against Nisumbha and Sumbha. After a tremendous struggle, she killed them both. Finally the Earth was cleansed of the demons' evil influence, and natural order was restored. Durga-Kali withdrew to the celestial realm, but she promised that even in her fierce form, she would protect and nourish her faithful worshippers.

The warlike goddess took her name after she saved the world by defeating a demon called Durga. Like Mahishasura, Durga had driven the gods from heaven and caused havoc on Earth by disrupting the natural order—rivers burst their banks, flooding fields and dwellings alike, heavy rains thrashed the lands and crops grew wildly out of season, while terrified *brahmins* neglected their study of the holy *Vedas*. Desperate, the gods appealed to Shiva, who told them to petition his wife, Devi. As soon as she heard about the plight of the Earth, she sent a beautiful creature named Kalaratiri ("Dark Night") to confront Durga. The demon's first army was defeated by Devi's ally, but when a second was sent into battle, she fled.

This time Devi herself went into battle. One thousand arms grew on her sacred body, and nine million emanations came forth to back her up in battle. The demon Durga ripped up a mountain and hurled it at her, but with her flailing sword she cut it into seven pieces and with a sure aim shot them all down with arrows. Durga then took the form of an elephant, but Devi sliced it up with her sharp nails. And when the demon became a fierce buffalo, she pierced it with her trident. Durga was forced back into his original form, and she wrestled him to the ground and killed him by plunging an arrow into his chest. In honor of this famous victory, she took the vanquished demon's name.

101

The Daughter of the Mountains

Shiva was distraught and inconsolable at the loss of Sati, but she returned to him as Parvati, daughter of Himavan, spirit god of the Himalaya mountains.

After a punishing journey through the towering Himalayas, the sage Narada paid a visit to the mountain god Himavan. He prophesied that Himavan's daughter would marry the great god Shiva. Pleased at the prospect, Himavan arranged for Parvati to wait on Shiva high in the mountains. But Shiva was too preoccupied with his searingly powerful meditation to take notice of the beautiful maiden.

At this time, the gods, who had been driven from heaven by a demon named Taraka, learned from Brahma that only a son of Shiva could save them. So they sent the love god Kama to awaken Shiva's interest in Parvati, hoping he would then produce an heir. Although Kama did hit home with his arrow and made Shiva notice Parvati, the love god also awoke Shiva's anger and was consumed by fire (see page 47). Shiva, wounded by Kama's arrow of love, looked longingly at Parvati for a few moments, but he quickly regained his self-control and settled once again to his meditation.

Now Parvati decided that if her beauty could not seduce the great god, she would turn to religious austerities in the hope of winning Shiva's heart. She settled in a grove near the peak on which he meditated and tried through rigorous self-denial to escape the rule of her physical senses. She starved herself of food, froze her body in icy pools and slept with nothing but the hard mountain ground as a bed. One day a wandering priest passed by, and seeing the fair young goddess engaged in such austere pursuits, stopped in the grove to talk to her. He asked her why she was being so hard on her beautiful flesh and laughed when she said she was

Shiva with Parvati as golden-skinned Uma, 10th-century copper-gilt inlay from Nepal.

performing austerities because she had set her heart on marrying the lord Shiva. The priest began to deride Shiva, calling him a foul-smelling hermit beggar who wore snakes wrapped around his body and daubed his skin with ashes. Parvati said she loved Shiva for all his oddities. Then the priest mocked Shiva again as a quick-tempered haunter of cemeteries. Parvati could stand no more and covered her ears, but in that instant the priest revealed himself as Shiva in disguise. The god said that he had been moved by her devotion, and he begged Parvati to be his wife if her father would allow it. Shiva and Parvati were soon married, and the gods were overjoyed, believing that now a warrior would be born who could rid the world of Taraka.

A Matter of Love and Death

After the fire of Shiva's third eye destroyed the love god Kama, the Earth became a barren place.
But, as Kama lay dead, the love god's faithful wife Rati persuaded Parvati to help.

Parvati begged Shiva to bring Kama back to life, and he was reborn on Earth as Pradyumna, a son of Krishna and his favorite wife Rukmini. But he was snatched from his cot by the demon Shambhara, who had been warned that the child would one day murder him, and was thrown into the sea.

Pradyumna was swallowed by a fish. The fish was then caught, and Shambhara unwittingly bought it at the market. That night his wife, Mayavati, prepared the dinner. And when she gutted the fish, she found the child inside.

Now, Mayavati was an incarnation of Rati, and as she stood in the kitchen she had a vision of the sage Narada who told her that the baby was her husband Kama. He then enabled her to make the boy invisible so she could raise him in secret.

When Pradyumna was young she tried to seduce him, but he was unwilling, for he believed her to be his mother. Mayavati then explained to Pradyumna that their souls were those of Rati and Kama. Soon they were lovers, and Mayavati became pregnant. When Shambhara began to mistreat her, Pradyumna attacked and killed the demon. Pradyumna and Mayavati then lived as man and wife, but later Pradyumna was killed in a fight. Back in the celestial realm, he resumed his form as Kama and faithful Rati came quickly to join him.

Shambhara throws the child Pradyumna into the ocean to rid himself of his future assassin. Little does he know that the child will return to haunt him.

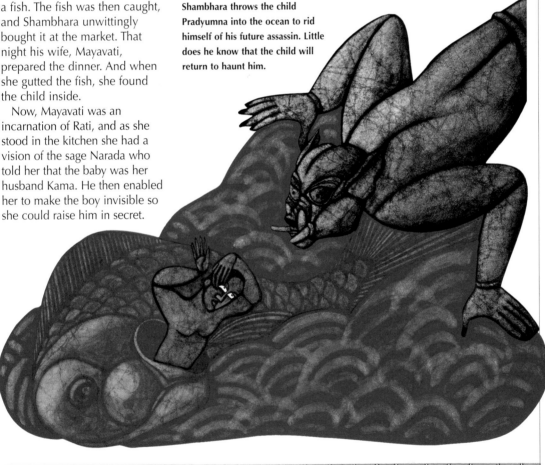

A Child to Save the Gods

Shiva and Parvati had a great love for each other, but for many years they did not produce a son. The gods, still desperate to be rid of Taraka, sent Agni, the fire god, to see Shiva in the Himalayas. His arrival interrupted Shiva and Parvati as they were making love, and when Agni complained that the gods were longing for a child, Shiva took some of his seed and threw it on to the ground. Agni at once transformed himself into a bird and gobbled it up, then flew off to find Indra.

Agni's belly burned fiercely, and the fire god had to drop the seed he had eaten. It fell into the sacred Ganges, but the river could not contain it either and threw the seed out into the rushes along its banks. There it settled, and it was transformed into a beautiful baby boy, luminous as the moon.

Six heavenly nymphs came to the river to perform their devotions and found the baby, who looked up lovingly at them. All the young women were overcome with longing for the boy, and they began to squabble over him. But the child developed six heads with six mouths, so all six women could suckle him. On that day the sound of drums was heard in heaven, and flower petals fell gently from the sky to indicate the gods' approval. High in the Himalayas, Shiva and Parvati felt an unexplained joy, and Parvati found milk flowing from her breasts. In time the child, Karttikeya, was brought to Parvati, who raised him as her own son. In later life, he became a great warrior and fulfilled Brahma's will by defeating the demon Taraka.

There are many different versions of the birth of Karttikeya, most emphasizing the power of Shiva's seed, which was too strong for lesser gods to carry. In the Shaivite version related in the *Shiva Purana* (which was compiled between the eighth and fourteenth centuries CE), all the gods travelled to the Himalayas to remind Shiva of the need for a child, and all ate his seed when he cast it on the ground. None, however, could bear it, and they had to vomit it up. Agni then carried some away and impregnated the wives of seven sages. But the sages' wives were abandoned by their husbands, who were angry at their mysterious pregnancies. The seven women produced just one embryo between them, which they then left in the Himalayas. The power of Shiva, which fed the growing child, was too great for the mountains, and they cast it into the Ganges. The river could not bear the infant's power either and cast it out on to the bank, where it was transformed into a handsome boy.

Peacocks, such as this 14th-century bronze Deccan example, were favorite images in early Hindu art. They represented immortality and acted as mounts for many gods including Karttikeya, god of war, who rode a peacock named Paravani.

Shiva, Parvati and their first son Karttikeya rest at home on Mount Kailasa. The holy family are often shown in a setting of domestic bliss, although persuading Shiva to raise a family, and provide a son to kill the demon Taraka, proved far from easy.

Karttikeya became the Hindu god of war and leader of the celestial army. He has twelve arms and six heads and is usually shown riding a peacock named Paravani. He is often described as a bachelor and thought of as a god of chastity. In some versions of the myth, he is the son of Agni rather than of Shiva. These accounts tell how Agni made love to Swaha, a daughter of the sage Daksha. She took his seed and placed it in sacred Ganges water, where it grew into a baby.

Shiva's role as god of the *lingam* often conflicts with his ascetic guise, in which his goal is to escape passion. This tension, however, not only shows his ability to combine opposites, but also illustrates his dependence on the female sex. He is often described making love to Parvati: in the version of Skanda's birth told in the *Shiva Purana*, Shiva's erotic exertions were so energetic that the other gods feared that the universe would be shaken to pieces. But his lovemaking with Parvati was often interrupted, and neither of his children was born by natural means from Parvati's womb.

Shiva's and Parvati's second son was the elephant-headed god Ganesha, a very popular object of worship. There are many different stories describing his birth and explaining how he came by his unusual appearance. One of the most popular tells how Parvati grew tired of Shiva's habit of walking in on her when she was bathing and so fashioned a child from soap suds to stand guard at the door and stop the god from entering. When Shiva arrived, he did not know who the child was; he flew into a fury when the boy tried to block his entrance and, seizing a sword, cut off the child's head. Parvati heard the noise and leapt from the bath. She came running out, and when she saw her son's headless body she wept and wailed at Shiva. The god took pity on his consort and promised her that he would cut off the head of the first animal he saw and use it to repair her son's body. At that moment, an elephant passed by and Shiva kept his word, decapitating the animal and placing its giant head on the boy's neck. Parvati was entranced by her son's odd but charming appearance.

Another version tells how, when Parvati begged Shiva for a son, he told her that as an ascetic he had no desire for children. She continued to pester him, however, and he made her a son from the red cloth of her gown. He was making fun of her, she thought, but her desire for a child was so great that she remolded the cloth baby and brought it to life. She hugged the baby boy and suckled him. Overcome with love, she wept tears of joy. But when Shiva took the child in his arms, the baby's head fell off.

105

Parvati was distraught and she would not let Shiva rest until he promised to bring her boy back to life. Shiva sent his bull Nandi to find a new head, and on his travels through the Earth and heavens, Nandi encountered Indra's great elephant Airavata. He tried to cut off its head, but Indra and his fellow gods came forward to defend the beast. Nandi, however, was too strong for them and took the head back to Shiva. In their heroic struggle, one of Airavata's tusks was broken off. When Shiva placed the elephant head on the boy's shoulders, a beautiful four-armed god with three eyes and a splendid pot belly came into being. Indra came to Shiva to beg forgiveness for having been unwilling to give up his elephant to make Shiva happy. Shiva accepted his repentance and told Indra to cast Airavata's headless corpse into the ocean, predicting that one day Airavata would rise again from the waters with a new head (see page 38).

Child of the Ocean

In their married life, the couple had many quarrels. After one, Parvati left her husband and performed such remarkable austerities that she was remade in dual form as the golden-skinned Uma and the terrifying black-skinned Kali. Another quarrel began when Shiva found that Parvati had fallen asleep while he was reading to her from the holy *Vedas*. He was involved in a complex explanation of ritual, and it enraged him that she had lost her concentration. But when Shiva reprimanded her, she

Shiva lost Parvati after an argument over her religious devotion. He won her back after defeating a shark that had been eating the fish in the coastal village she was staying in. Watercolor from a copy of the *Gita Govinda*, Mewar, Rajasthan, c. 1550.

denied that she had been sleeping and said that she had simply closed her eyes to help her think. Shiva tested her by asking a question about the scriptures he had been reading, and Parvati could not answer. Then he cursed his wife to leave the Himalayas and be born a mortal.

With Parvati gone, Shiva sat down eagerly to resume his meditation, but he found that the image of her delightful body disturbed his concentration. The more he tried to cast her from his mind the stronger the fascination grew, and eventually he resolved to get her back. On Earth Parvati had been born in an Indian coastal village where the people made their living by fishing. Her beauty made the young men of the village view her with awe, and she had no offers of marriage.

Shiva sent his bull attendant Nandi to Earth to track Parvati down, and he took the form of a fierce shark scouring the coastal waters. He discovered Parvati in the village and began to haunt the sea nearby, eating the fish and tearing the fishermen's nets to shreds. The poor seamen were facing ruin. They had caught a few glimpses of the shark, and in the stories they told each other it grew bigger and fiercer with every telling. They were too frightened to challenge this beast of the sea themselves, but they announced that whoever could rid them of it would win the hand of Parvati, the most beautiful maiden on the coast.

When Shiva heard this, he descended to Earth and disguised himself as a fisherman. In the blue coastal waters, he was able to subdue Nandi, and he dragged the shark back to the village behind his boat. Parvati recognized her lord and they were married. The village men and women said farewell to the couple, and Shiva and Parvati travelled back to their home in the Himalayas.

The Cult of Ganesha

Parvati's son Ganesha, the plump elephant-headed god, is the center of a popular cult. He brings good fortune to all kinds of activity.

Hindus number Ganesha among the five most important gods—with Brahma, Vishnu, Shiva and Devi. His combination of animal and human attributes is said to reflect the merging of qualities that occurs when a worshipper's soul achieves unity with the divine.

Ganesha is a god of beginnings. His image stands at the entrances of houses and temple sanctuaries, where he acts as a protector. He is always honored first, before devotees embark on their worship of other gods. He has the power to do away with obstacles, and those who worship him make offerings to win his favor for any project they are about to undertake—from composing a letter to making a journey or constructing a new building.

Writers often invoke his name at the start of books because he is a god of wisdom and is also renowned as a skilled scribe. His elephant's head and the rat or mouse on which he rides are emblems of sagacity, and it is said that he wrote down the *Mahabharata* at the dictation of the scribe Vsaya. Before beginning, he made Vsaya promise never to stop and never to use words that were difficult to follow, which explains the accessible quality of the epic.

Ganesha's name means "Lord of Hosts," and another of his roles is as the general of Shiva's army. He has a pot belly because of his great fondness for sweets and fruits, which are his favorite offerings. One of his tusks was broken off when his head was taken from Airavata (see main text), and he carries it in one of his four hands. He is said to use the tusk as a writing implement.

As god of wisdom and good fortune, Ganesha is always worshipped before all other gods. The marigolds and lotuses that adorn this marble statue in southern India have been given as offerings to him, and sometimes the sweets that gave him his pot belly are included too.

Parvati's Golden Skin

A lovers' quarrel between Shiva and his black-skinned goddess, Parvati, brought about their separation. She left their mountain home in a fury, intent on performing austerities that would win her the boon of a golden skin to satisfy her companion.

High in the Himalayas, Shiva jested with Parvati, embracing her and speaking softly. Her skin was so dark, he said, that when she laid herself against his pale body, it was like a black snake climbing a sandalwood tree. Parvati pulled sharply away, and anger made her eyes glow red. Shiva quickly tried to calm the goddess, withdrawing what he had said, but she continued to rail at him. Soon Shiva himself grew angry, and as the lovers traded insults Parvati declared that if her body was so loathsome, she would abandon it through meditation.

Parvati then left, her anger blazing. On her way from Shiva's Himalayan home, she instructed Nandi to guard her husband's door and not let any other women in—for she knew his nature well. She told him she was going to practice asceticism in order to gain a golden skin. Her son Ganesha begged to go with her, and they set out together.

On the way they met a mountain goddess named Kusamamodini. Parvati asked her to keep watch over Shiva's palace and warn her if any other woman went in to see the great god. Kusamamodini promised to do as she was asked, and Parvati and Ganesha continued on their way until they found a perfect place to practice austerities. Then the goddess lost herself in meditation while the elephant-headed boy guarded her.

This 20th-century gouache shows Parvati with golden skin. Although this form reflects a softer aspect of the goddess, it was acquired in anger, after the goddess had argued with her husband.

The moment Parvati was gone, a demon by the name of Adi made his way to Shiva's palace. Adi's father, Andhaka, had been hurt by Shiva, and Adi was seeking revenge. Adi found Nandi standing sentry at Shiva's door, but he slipped past the bull by taking the form of a slithering serpent. Then he stepped into Shiva's bedchamber in the form of a golden goddess. Shiva hurried to embrace the woman, for he was thrilled by her perfect form and complexion, and he thought that she was Parvati returned from her devotions. But as he talked to her and embraced her he became suspicious. He examined her body closely, but he could not find the lotus mark that Parvati had on her left side. Then Shiva knew that Adi was a demon. Summoning the power of his anger, he dispatched Adi with the spite that he deserved.

Meanwhile Kusamamodini had used a mountain breeze to send news to Parvati that Shiva had been seduced by a golden-skinned visitor. Parvati grew mad with jealousy and anger, and from her mouth her fury emerged in the form of a lion. But then Brahma came softly pacing across the mountainside and asked Parvati what she desired, as he was the giver of boons and her austerities had been great indeed. She said that she wanted a golden skin, because her husband had mocked her. And Brahma then granted her wish.

The Devotees of Death

For hundreds of years until the mid-1800s, assassins called thuggees robbed and murdered travellers in central and northern India—and sacrificed them to the goddess Kali.

The *thuggees*' preferred way of killing their victims was garroting—a method they said had been taught to them by Kali herself using a clay dummy. They would befriend travellers on the road, and then turn on them and strangle them with a noose or handkerchief. On the sacred Ganges River between Benares and Calcutta, they posed as boatmen, offering to take pilgrims across the water—but when far from shore they would rob and kill their victims.

On the Ganges, the victims were generally thrown into the water, but on land the corpses were buried in pits ritually dug using a sacred pickax. One third of the robbery proceeds, as well as the bodies, were offered to Kali, in curious rituals that included sacrifices of sugar to the goddess. All the victims were men, as the goddess did not desire female sacrifices.

The cult of Kali lives on in the form of painting known as Kaligat. The style, demonstrated in this 19th-century image, still thrives today, focusing on lurid representations of the avenging black-faced goddess.

The movement took its name from the Sanskrit *sthaga,* or thief. The *thuggees'* origins, however, are not known. Some members were Muslims, and they claimed to be descended from seven different Muslim tribes. Some accounts say they were preying on innocent pilgrims and travellers as long ago as the seventh century CE.

The British authorities made a concerted effort to stamp out the *thuggee* movement during the governorship of Lord William Bentinck (1834–1835), and more than 3,000 were captured in the 1830s. By 1861, *thuggees* were a thing of the past, but they left one lasting legacy in the form of the word "thug," meaning a violent criminal.

Goddess of Good Fortune

Another form taken by the Great Goddess was Lakshmi, wife of Vishnu. She is still worshipped under the name Sri, goddess of beauty, prosperity and good fortune, and she has long been associated with the principal gods. In the *Vedas*, Sri was wife of Varuna, chief of the gods, and sometimes of the golden-haired sun god, Surya.

Lakshmi emerged from the Milk Ocean when the gods churned it to produce *amrita,* and she at once became Vishnu's consort (see box, page 38). In most accounts, she was originally the daughter of a sage named Bhrigu, but she hid in the ocean after the gods were driven out of heaven.

She is pictured as an ideal of slim-waisted, full-breasted feminine beauty. In some accounts of the churning of the Milk Ocean, when she emerged —one of fourteen precious things that were the happy by-products of the process—both Shiva and Vishnu were entranced by her beauty and disputed the right to marry her. But because Shiva had already claimed the moon when it rose from the ocean, Vishnu took Lakshmi. Shiva was so upset that he swallowed the poison that was produced during the churning and so saved the whole of creation.

As Vishnu's *shakti*, or energy, she played an enabling role in his acts of protection and preservation. Some Vaishnavites conceive of god and goddess linked as Lakshmi-Narayana, together forming the personal and approachable face of *brahman*. When Vishnu took flesh as the upholder of *dharma*, she also incarnated as his companion. She was the devoted, ever-faithful Sita when Vishnu was born as righteous Rama, and when the god became Krishna, Lakshmi was both the passionate and beautiful cowgirl, Radha, and Krishna's favorite wife Rukmini. Their union is seen as an image of the soul's relationship with god.

Male devotees of Vishnu sometimes dress as women in order to gain greater spiritual intimacy with the deity. Towards the end of his life, the renowned sixteenth-century mystic Sri Caitanya identified more and more strongly with Radha and regularly wore women's clothes. Mystery surrounds his death as he is said to have simply disappeared, but his followers claimed he had been a full incarnation of Vishnu's eighth avatar, Krishna.

In the myth of the churning of the Milk Ocean, Vishnu assumed female form to become the bewitchingly beautiful Mohini, who seduced the demons into giving up the *amrita* after they had snatched it from the gods.

Bringer of Wealth and Fertility

As Sri, Lakshmi is said to reside in sweet-smelling floral garlands, which bring fortune and wealth to the wearer. But because good fortune can disappear as quickly as it appears—and despite her great faithfulness as Sita—Lakshmi is sometimes referred to as changeable or fickle, and her good will is eagerly sought.

She also has a role as a fertility goddess and is particularly linked to the richness of the soil. Because of this, she is sometimes known as Karisin ("rich in dung"), a variation that is naturally popular in the countryside.

The love god Kama was Lakshmi's son, fruit of her union with Vishnu. She is particularly associated with the lotus flower, a common symbol of fertility (see box, page 113), and another of her names is Padma, which means "Lotus." She is shown either seated or upright on a lotus, sometimes with Vishnu. In the popular image of Vishnu reclining on the serpent Ananta, Lakshmi is depicted soothing her lord by rubbing his feet with ointments. Her image is usually golden-skinned.

Lakshmi and the Washerwoman

This tale is told about the autumn festival of lights, Diwali, which is held in Lakshmi's honor. Householders light lamps to attract the benevolent goddess to their home; if she visits, they believe she will bring them prosperity in the coming year.

One year, at Diwali, the king of a northern Indian realm gave his wife the most wonderful necklace of pearls. But when she went for her morning swim, leaving her necklace and clothes by the shore, a crow swooped down from the sky and snatched the precious pearls.

To comfort his distraught wife, the king at once dispatched his servants to announce a generous reward for their return.

The crow, meanwhile, had dropped the necklace over the poorest part of a city, and it had been found by a washerwoman. When she heard the desperate proclamations about the reward, she made her way to the palace, where she proudly handed the necklace to the king.

He was delighted with the woman's honesty and offered her a purse heavy with coins as a reward. But the woman refused. Instead, she asked the king to grant her a favor. That night, when the celebrations for Diwali were due to begin, she wanted her humble hut to be the only lighted house in the kingdom. She asked the king to forbid the lighting of any other Diwali lamps for this one night. It seemed a small thing to the king, who did not take Diwali very seriously anyway, so he willingly granted the washerwoman her wish.

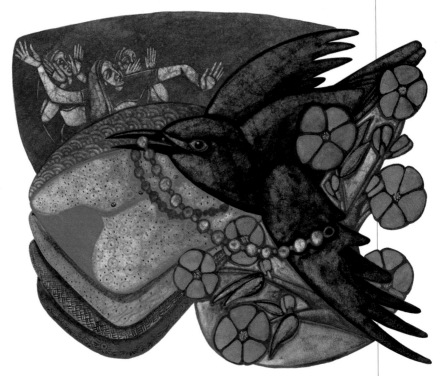

The queen cries out as a passing crow flies off with the precious pearl necklace she had left with her clothes as she went for her morning swim.

But Lakshmi was not pleased when she came to the kingdom to inspect the displays of Diwali lamps. At first she thought no one had bothered to light any lamps at all, but then she saw the washerwoman's house in the distance. She walked swiftly there and knocked on the door. The washerwoman greeted her, but would let the goddess inside only if she promised to stay for seven generations.

Lakshmi was pleased that the woman was so devoted to her, and she agreed. On that day the washerwoman's luck changed, and she was never to know poverty again. Her sons and daughters, and their children and their offspring, enjoyed lasting prosperity and good fortune— the gift of Lakshmi—for seven long generations.

Mistress of the Land

Away from large city-based temples, the Great Goddess is worshipped in a seemingly endless number of forms at folk shrines across India. Every area and village has its own deity or deities, most of whom are feminine.

In rural areas of India, people rely on the land in much the same way as they did in 3000 BCE, and folk religion remains focused on keeping the land fertile. The goddess, bringer of fertil-ity, can be worshipped anywhere: in the land itself, in mountains, rocks, fields, plants, trees and rivers. In the state of Tamil Nadu in southeast India, Devi takes the name Mariyamman, consid-ered like Durga-Kali to be a warrior and propitiated as a protectress of vil-lages and families. She is also wor-shipped in the form of trees and snakes. Hindu deities are said to divide into "hot" and "cool." The hot ones—including fierce aspects of Devi such as Durga and Kali and many village goddesses—are linked to disease, fertility and violent passion. The cool ones include male gods such as Vishnu and benevolent aspects of Devi such as Lakshmi and Parvati; they represent the escape from passion in spiritual detachment. In many ways hot and cool are divided according to social caste. The cool

deities are linked to urban temples, where they are venerated in iconic form and served by *brahmin* priests. Hot ones are worshipped primarily outside temples, at simple shrines consisting of no more than a pile of rocks or a tree and served by non-*brahmin* priests or priestesses. Generally, cool deities receive simple vegetarian offerings, such as fruit, whereas hot ones demand blood sacrifices of goats or even buffaloes. Sometimes, as in the case of Mariyamman, a deity can actually have both hot and cool aspects. She is worshipped in a cool, iconic form in temples but also accepts blood sac-rifice at country shrines. It is another aspect of the eclectic nature of Hinduism that the myriad folk cults exist alongside the more formal and sophisti-cated temple worship.

Bengal in eastern India is rich in local deities. Prime among them is the serpent Manasa, goddess of snakes. She is the sister of Shesha, the serpent of eternity, and is worshipped for her power to save devotees from snake bites.

Manasa once persecuted a merchant, named Chando, for years because he refused to propitiate her as a goddess. The merchant was a committed devotee of Shiva who, as a boon, had granted him the power to perform magic. But despite this pro-tection, Manasa continued to harass him. Her cam-paign of destruction grew ever worse. She bit all of

A snake-goddess winds herself around a pillar of the 11th-century Bhubaneshwar temple in Orissa. Snakes were symbols of life and fertility and, because of their ability to shed their skin, of immortality. Their friendship had to be secured by sacrifices.

his sons, and they died from her poison; she then ruined his business. Chando made a new home, built up a new business and had another son, Lakshmindra. His life was at last peaceful, until his son married a young woman named Behula. Manasa saw her chance; on the night of their marriage, a snake bit Lakshmindra.

Chando, crazed with grief, determined to find someone who could revive his son. He put the body on a raft and sent it off downstream. Behula went with it, and when she saw a mother bring her dead son back to life, she asked for help. The mother led Behula to Manasa, who promised to revive Lakshmindra if Behula pledged to make Chando worship her. She agreed and travelled home with her revived husband, telling Chando on her arrival that the young couple would come into his house only if he would abandon his proud resistance and worship Manasa. Chando, delighted at seeing his son again, gave in.

The Lotus Flower

The lotus is a popular feature of Indian statuary and architecture. An object of great beauty, the lotus is also a symbol of creativity and perfection.

The lotus often appears in sacred images as a throne for a god or goddess. When Brahma arises from Vishnu's navel before the creation of the universe, he sits on a lotus flower whose stalk connects him to Vishnu; Sarasvati, goddess of the creative arts, is often shown resting on one.

Lakshmi is particularly associated with this flower. When Vishnu came to Earth as the dwarf Vamana, she emerged from the waters floating on a lotus. In the version of the demoness Putana's attempt to kill Krishna told in the *Bhagavata Purana*, she appears in Krishna's village carrying a lotus, and this made the villagers think she must be an incarnation of Lakshmi. The lotus is used as a symbol of fertility, representing the richness of the Earth and sometimes the *yoni*. It is also a symbol of the manifested form of the universe, arising from the chaos of the cosmic waters.

The lotus is a common feature of Hindu art. The 16th-century earthenware carving (*above*) is from Guar, Bengal. This detail (*below*) is from a musicological text from Rajasthan, *c.* 1760.

THE LIVING GODDESS

Prehistoric worship in India was founded on the cults of fertility and the Mother Goddess. While male deities came to dominate religious belief in most other cultures, the veneration of female energy remains central to Hindu ritual. No Hindu god can function without his female consort, and the thousands of local folk deities found throughout the Indian countryside are mostly female.

One figure dominates goddess worship, however: Kali the merciless destroyer, whose power gives life to the universe, activates the potential of the gods and rids the world of demons intent on bringing chaos to the harmonious structure of the cosmos.

Top Left: **This shrine at Gwalior in Uttar Pradesh shelters an archetypal image of *shakti*, female energy, images of which are common in the countryside. There is no recognizable female form, only a smooth block of stone, covered in crimson paste signifying femininity. On to this are pasted strips of silver foil reflecting the fact that *devi*, the general term for *shakti*, derives from the Sanskrit *div*, which means "to shine."**

Above: **A stone statue of Kali stands in a clearing in a forest in Bihar, in north-eastern India. In this part of India, the form of goddess worshipped is the black-skinned Mahavidya Kali, who has been the center of a cult since the 15th century or earlier.**

Above: **Among the oldest artifacts in India are figures of an ancient Mother Goddess, like this 3rd-century BCE grey terracotta example from Mathura. Evidence for the worship of female deities can be traced back to c. 3000 BCE.**

Left: **This 18th-century diagram from a *Hatha Yoga* textbook shows an *asana*, or divine position, which recalls the *yonic* triangle. The hole in the rock behind, and the lotus flowers in the foreground, complete the female imagery.**

Right: **The goddess remains a central focus of worship for men across India. Many seek unity with her by adopting her likeness. Here a devotee dresses as Kali for the festival procession to the Bhagavati temple in Kerala.**

MASTERS OF ENLIGHTENMENT

No trace remains of Meghavarna's vast monastery at Bodh Gaya. The magnificent Mahabodhi temple, one of the most sacred sites of one of the world's most ancient religions, the spot upon which the Buddha first attained true enlightenment, would still be an overgrown ruin had it not been for the recent intervention of, largely foreign, enthusiasts. History has dealt harshly with Indian Buddhism: the Hindu persecutions of the early medieval period were followed by an Islamic invasion in the twelfth century, which saw monuments razed and patronage co-opted. Less traumatically, yet every bit as thoroughly, an ascendant Hinduism was meanwhile absorbing key Buddhist myths, rituals and even adherents. For much of the modern era, Buddhism was largely extinct in India, dispersed into small pockets and surviving best at the subcontinent's outermost extremities in Nepal and Sri Lanka.

Buddhism would appear to be at home among the high hills of Kathmandu, that kingdom in the sky where its originator was born. Yet it was not here, in the peaceful, pleasant atmosphere of his own native country, that the Buddha was to found his faith some 2,500 years ago, but down below in the populous lowlands to the south. Peasant farmers tilled every inch of these sun-scorched plains, while teeming cities crowded to the banks of the Ganges. Here, in what amounted to a bustling commercial corridor between the rich kingdoms of east and west, the traffic in ideas was no less frenetic. Along a river long-since sacred to Hindus, rival religions clashed and jostled for advantage. Itself a multiplicity of sparring sects, Hinduism had to hold its corner in a struggle for spiritual survival that left none of its participants unmarked. Hinduism, Jainism, Buddhism, Islam, Sikhism and Christianity all influenced one another over the centuries. This maelstrom slowly settled down to become a confrontation between the forces of Hinduism and Islam; Indian Buddhism would end up a casualty, while Jainism would for a long time be marginalized. Both, however, survived and emerged in their different ways at once strengthened and enriched.

Opposite: A 5th-century sandstone head of the Buddha from the ancient site of Sarnath, north of Varanasi, an important Buddhist center.

Below: A late 18th-century Jain votive painting on paper showing three of the 24 Jain apostles, or *tirthankaras.*

117

The Birth of the Buddha

Strange portents attended the birth of the Buddha, mysterious hints at greatness to come. The son of a noble warrior and a royal princess, Gautama Siddhartha grew up in privilege and luxury. But such comforts were as nothing to him compared with the beauty of truth.

The boy who was destined to be the Buddha was born in the foothills of the Himalayas, in what is now the province of Terai. His father was a noble warrior, Suddhodana, the king of Kapilavastu, head of the Gautama clan of the Shakya tribe; his mother, Mahayama, was a royal princess. One night, as Mahayama slept peacefully in the royal palace, a great white elephant came to her bedside and entered her womb. As the months went by, a desire for solitude and silence came increasingly upon her, and finally she took herself off into the forest where she could meditate alone. Lying down beneath a sal tree, she finally gave birth, not to an infant but to a miniature man, the future Buddha. Where his foot first touched the ground, the earth thrust forth a lotus plant, and as he looked about him to each of the points of the compass, gods, goddesses, men, women and demons saluted his sanctity. Eighty thousand joyful relations flocked together to celebrate his coming, and at a splendid ceremony he was given the name of Siddhartha. A hundred and eight *brahmins* were present to bless his birth, and 100 godmothers promised her their help. Overwhelmed by her joy, her life's dearest ambitions all accomplished, Queen Mahayama died only two days later, to be reborn among the deities. Siddhartha was looked after by his mother's sister, the princess Prajapati.

Buddhas mark the entrance to the Swayambunath temple, near Kathmandu, the place where Siddhartha emerged from the lotus flower to take his first steps on his road to buddhahood. Several hundred steps lead from this gateway to a temple beyond.

It was prophesied that the boy would become a buddha, or "Enlightened One," but Suddhodana had ambitions of worldly glory for his son. As long as he protected the boy from ever seeing the unhappiness of human life, his advisers told him, Siddhartha would accept his royal destiny without question. Suddhodana accordingly built three special palaces for his son, and here the pampered prince grew up in unimaginable luxury, lulled by soft music, delighted by gentle fragrances, his every wish anticipated by 1,000 willing servitors. So, ignorant of his true destiny, the young Siddhartha grew from boyhood to youth, his education that of a future king.

As Siddhartha emerged into manhood, a rivalry developed with his cousin and companion Devadatta. One day Dandapani, father of the lovely Yasodhara, Siddhartha's intended bride, demanded that the young prince prove himself in manly arts. A tournament was arranged, in which Siddhartha might match his skill, strength and intellect against those of Devadatta and another young warrior, Sundarnand. Devadatta strove implacably to outdo the young prince, and as the tournament started, he went all out to win in every event. Yet Siddhartha was not only victorious in the more artistic events such as music, mathematics, elocution and recitation, but also outdid his more warlike rival as horseman and charioteer. In archery, and even in wrestling, he held Devadatta to a draw. Only in the fencing contest did Devadatta at last prevail. It seemed natural that Siddhartha would be awarded the garland, but when he was, Devadatta looked on in outrage.

Siddhartha's sense of well-being was only enhanced by the joys of matrimony. Guards kept the realities of the outside world at bay, while within the palace walls were only luxury and pleasure. Increasingly concerned that Siddhartha might come to look beyond his blissful confinement, Suddhodana had the royal apartments filled with beautiful women, poetry, music and every kind of delight. So it was that the young prince reached a man's years without ever so much as dreaming that existence might have its less agreeable

A Divine Cosmology

The form of the Buddhist cosmos was of little interest to a mind focused on an abstract state of enlightenment beyond mere Earthly concerns. Yet the faith's rapidly-growing following required a less rarefied way of grasping its salient points. And into the vacuum left by "pure" Buddhism spilled innumerable influences from Hinduism and Jainism.

At the center of the Buddhist universe, Mount Meru rises from an endless plain. Beneath lie 136 hells, each marked out for the punishment of a particular sin. Mount Meru's peak provides the foundation for the realms of the Four Great Kings, Dhritarashtra, Virudhaka, Virupaksha and Kubera, who rule the east, the south, the west and the north. Above these kingdoms lies the heaven of Shakra, the Buddhist equivalent of the Hindu god Indra. There are forty-four additional heavens, each with its own deities and delights for rewarding virtue, and beyond these lie the heavens' topmost tiers: where buddhas dwell in abstract formlessness, having transcended time and self.

Above: Rooftop decorations stand before the *stupa* at Bodnath, Kathmandu, one of Buddhism's holiest shrines.

119

aspects. In time, however, Siddhartha grew curious about what might lie beyond the walls of his palace. Ignoring his father's pleas, he resolved to visit the world outside. Guessing at his son's intentions, Suddhodana did his best to replicate his carefully contrived illusion in the city outside. He had the streets surrounding the palace all scrupulously swept, and the facades of their buildings appealingly decorated. Any sick, aged or ugly people, and any sight that might rock the unquestioning complacency of his son was banished from the vicinity. Yet the gods did not wish the king's sleight to succeed: Siddhartha's outings from the palace were to change him forever. In all, he would make four excursions in the course of which he would see the "Four Sights." The first of these was a stooped, wizened man, shuffling awkwardly along with the aid of a stick. This, his charioteer Chandaka told the astonished prince, was the appearance of old age. All human beings were destined to this decrepitude, he said, even the youthful Siddhartha. On their next outing, the pair found the beauties of the city scene disfigured by another sight of suffering: a man racked by disease and pain. This too, said Chandaka, could happen to anybody, even to a king's son such as Siddhartha. Still more shocking, however, was the sight of a corpse, encountered during their next excursion. Nothing had prepared the prince for the thought that his life must one day end. Filled

The Buddhist Pantheon

If the cosmos imagined by Buddhists reflects that of India's ancient Hindu tradition, so too does its array of deities.

All the great gods and goddesses of the Hindu tradition have their counterparts in popular Buddhism, though their names and their functions have often been changed. Hence the Hindu god Indra, supreme among deities, has his equivalent in Shakra, the heavenly king. Buddhists recognize the rule of the deathly Dharmaraja, or Yama, in the underworld, but demote the great Shiva and his wife Parvati to the role of doorkeepers to the Buddha. The Hindu earth god Kubera, renamed Jambhala, is bodyguard to the sage. Demons suck the 500 nipples of Jambhala's dreadful wife Hariti, terrifying both in her ferocity and her fertility. The goddesses of the Buddhist pantheon are not on the whole distinguished by their gentleness. The dawn goddess Marishi has none of the benignity of the Hindu Ushas. Not all the Buddhist deities are so terrible, however: Sarasvati, goddess of teaching, and Prajna, the goddess of knowledge, are kind. Nor, indeed, are they all borrowings from Hindu tradition. Tara has made the opposite transition. Once the "Mother of all the Buddhas," she has been absorbed into Hindu lore.

Left: A 10th-century stone image of Tara, mother of the buddhas, protector of people and bestower of long life. This "supreme mother" typically embodies wisdom and compassion as female attributes.

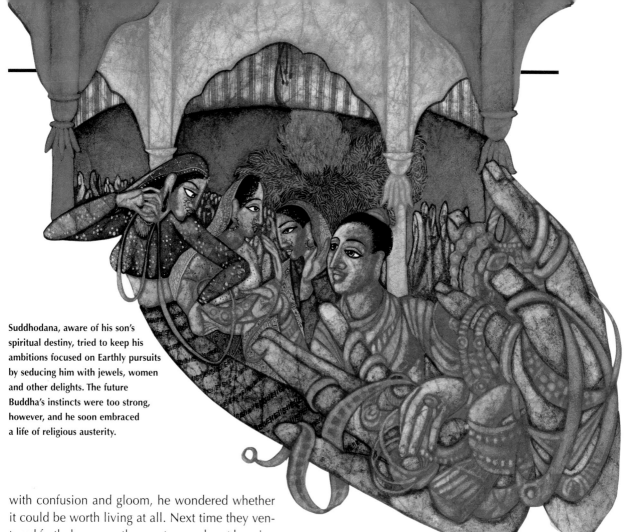

Suddhodana, aware of his son's spiritual destiny, tried to keep his ambitions focused on Earthly pursuits by seducing him with jewels, women and other delights. The future Buddha's instincts were too strong, however, and he soon embraced a life of religious austerity.

with confusion and gloom, he wondered whether it could be worth living at all. Next time they ventured forth, however, they met a monk out begging with his bowl. This man, said Chandaka, had willingly forsaken family, home and comfort in order to seek peace and spiritual fulfilment in a life of poverty and prayer. Moved beyond anything he had ever experienced by the sight of such unworldliness, Siddhartha returned home resolved to emulate the monk's example and to set out himself upon the road of renunciation. The luxuries of the palace seemed like nothing to him now, and although the sight of his sleeping wife and baby did tug at his heartstrings, he stiffened his resolve. He stepped briskly from their chamber, went out to where Chandaka was waiting with his horse Kanthaka and took off into the world.

Soon they came down beside the Anoma River, where Siddhartha took leave of his faithful charioteer. Taking off his royal jewels and his rich clothes, and cutting off his beautiful black hair, he handed them to Chandaka, bidding him to take

them back to his family at the palace, along with his farewell message. Siddhartha said he was setting off to seek an end to old age and suffering, and he would vanquish death or die himself in the attempt. If he were successful in his quest, he would return home in triumph.

For six years Siddhartha dedicated himself to asceticism. Yet no spiritual benefits seemed to flow from his suffering: the road to enlightenment seemed as elusive as ever. Instead, the *bodhisattva* (buddha in waiting) determined to pursue his own path, a "Middle Way," as he called it, between luxury and asceticism. Physical self-mortification, he realized, merely made an obsession of the hurting, hungering human flesh. Escape from the body and its preoccupations would require an inward, contemplative journey. So, accepting the gift of food

121

that a young woman gave him, he sat down beneath a tree, resolving to remain where he was until he had attained enlightenment. Alarmed to see that a new and irresistible heavenly enemy was at the point of coming into being, Mara, king of the demons, summoned up all his forces and gathered all his energies to prevent the *bodhisattva* from becoming a buddha. Mara hurled all the elements at his command at the holy man, but his evil was no match for the other's supreme good. His lightning bolts became lotus blossoms and wafted gently down around the peacefully praying Siddhartha; the clouds of earth and ashes he launched were turned by his enemy's righteousness into sweet-smelling sandalwood, while all the darkness Mara could muster could not dim the surpassing brightness of the *bodhisattva's* glowing soul. Thunder filled the heavens and the Earth shook, cleaving the universe. Mara and his demons fled in panic, leaving Gautama Siddhartha meditating still, the calm victor in possession of the field.

Their way now safe from evil spirits, a host of more benign gods and goddesses gathered to witness the *bodhisattva's* final transformation through *dhyana* or deep meditation. Through three long watches of the night, Siddhartha moved slowly by stages through the limits of Earthly reality. Finally, during the fourth watch, he saw how man's restless destiny might be transcended and freedom and stillness at last attained in a state of nirvana that extinguished all Earthly attachments as one might blow out a candle. The man's moment of extinction was the birth of the Buddha. In that ecstatic instant, Siddhartha saw the possibility of eternal salvation. But he did not seize it for himself. He decided that his place was in the world, among his fellow men and women. And so, starting with two merchants, with whom he shared a meal, the Buddha began to gather around him a group of disciples. Retracing his steps in the hope of recruiting the companions of his ascetic years, he found his way barred by the Ganges, and a ferryman who insisted on cash payment, which the Buddha was unable to provide. Undaunted, he flew across the mighty river, coming to earth on the other side,

The Bodh Gaya *stupa*, which marks the place where the Buddha achieved true enlightenment. The bodhi tree that grows at the site today is held to be a direct descendent of the pipal tree under which Siddhartha resisted Mara's onslaughts.

where he found his old companions still striving after salvation through self-abnegation and austerity. At first derisive, they soon became devoted disciples, persuaded despite themselves by the Buddha's insightful teaching and impressed by his miraculous powers. Soon hundreds and thousands were flocking to follow this great teacher. His quest successfully concluded, the Buddha could now keep his promise to his family, and return home to Kapilavastu. Yet his homecoming was not to be quite what his father had imagined. Begging for his bread in the streets of the city, the great prince was returning a monk. Suddhodana was at first appalled, but eventually he was won over by the Buddha's words of wisdom, and soon the whole royal family was converted.

But there remained people who distrusted Siddhartha's sacred message, and they found a ready leader in Devadatta, his boyhood rival. Devadatta dedicated himself to the task of bringing down his old enemy, but all his stratagems ended in failure. In despair, Devadatta fell seriously ill. When he recovered, he let it be thought that he had repented. He went to see the Buddha to ask for forgiveness, but his murderous intentions were apparent to the gods. Flames billowed forth from the ground and burned him up where he stood.

For forty-five years the Buddha's mission continued, but at last he decided that he had lived long enough. Making his way to the country of Mallas, he lay down in an enchanted grove. Great rulers gathered to take their leave of the teacher. He comforted them, explaining that his own work was now complete and that the rest would be up to them. Then he fell unconscious and died. Though men and minor deities mourned, the great gods rejoiced at the Buddha's passage to nirvana: they understood the necessity for this progression beyond the world. Deep darkness filled the sky, broken only by bolts of lightning. The Earth was thrown into tumult, and the rivers appeared to boil. His disciples built a pyre for their departed leader that burst into flames of its own accord at the moment the heavens appointed. When the flames had died down and the smoke cleared, his remains were divided up between eight princes, who set off to bear these sacred relics throughout the world. The Buddha's body may have departed in death, but his spirit endured among the living; his holy life may finally have been over, but a great world religion was only beginning.

The image of the reclining Buddha symbolizes parinirvana, the ultimate state of serenity achieved by the Buddha upon his death. This 12th-century statue is from Polonnaruwa in Sri Lanka.

The Buddha's 500 Faces

The founder and figurehead of Buddhism had lived through many existences in a wide variety of physical forms before he took on his final shape as Siddhartha, humankind's divine teacher, at some time in the sixth century BCE.

The stories of the *Jataka* present the past lives of the Buddha in myriad different manifestations: merchant or god, robber or vulture, antelope or deer. Since in each of these forms he attained the greatest perfection possible in that particular state, he was reincarnated anew at an ever higher level of existence. There are over 500 *Jataka* tales, each of which has entertained and enlightened readers for 2,000 years and more.

Fresh marigolds cover the footprints of the Buddha at Bodh Gaya, the place where he at last achieved enlightenment. The prints are set within stylized lotus petals, showing that they have risen from the flower of wisdom and purity.

In one celebrated story, the being destined to be the Buddha was born as the boy Mahasattva, the scion of a distinguished *brahmin* family. But this youth born to power and privilege chose to embrace poverty and prayer, renouncing his father's house to wander in the wilderness, gathering about him a body of disciples. The young *bodhisattva* would not swerve from the path of righteousness. Walking one day through a remote mountain wasteland, he came to a cave where he found a tigress, exhausted after giving birth. Scrawny and thin, she was maddened by starvation: her own newborn cubs were as enemies to her; she would devour them, it seemed, if it would prolong her own existence. The *bodhisattva* wondered if life could ever be worth such a price. Far from fearing the wretched animal, Mahasattva saw her as his own fellow creature and, knowing that the spirit was more important than the flesh, decided to help her in the only way he could. So, in front of his astonished disciples, he lay down before the ravening beast, bidding her spare her cubs and eat him instead. The tigress, fortified by this feast, lived on to recover her strength and to rear her young in safety. And the dead *bodhisattva*, perfected by this supreme self-sacrifice, had prepared himself to live again in a higher form.

The White Elephant

Once, the Buddha was reborn in the form of a white elephant Chadanta, splendidly arrayed with six long, gleaming tusks. He lived in the forest with his two beautiful elephant wives. Theirs was a happy existence in a lush and fertile kingdom where Chadanta proved a loving husband. But one wife could not rest in such felicity and resented having to share her husband, however attentive he might be.

Seething with jealousy towards her rival, she prayed to be reborn as a human princess. Her wish was duly granted and, blessed with great beauty and charm, she grew up to marry the king of Benares. One day she called together all her husband's huntsmen, and asked them to search in the forest for an elephant with six tusks. They were to capture and kill this prodigious beast, she told them, and bring back his fine tusks. The huntsmen set off, searching vainly for many days deep in the jungle, before one of the men, Sonuttara, found what they had sought—a fine bull elephant, with six long and shapely tusks. Quickly, he dug a pit in which to trap it, and soon Chadanta was captured.

As Sonuttara rained down arrows upon him, Chadanta asked why he wanted to kill him. Sonuttara told him of his queen's orders, and the poor elephant immediately understood all. He realized in a flash who the queen must be, and the smoldering resentment that must have motivated her malice. Accepting his fate, he even assisted Sonuttara in his deadly work. First he helped the huntsman to climb up his tusks so that he might cut them off at the root; then, when they proved

too tough to be cut by human force, he seized the saw with his own trunk and severed them himself, courteously offering his ivory booty to the awestruck Sonuttara while the lifeblood ebbed away from his mighty body. The huntsman went back to the queen with his astonishing story; when she heard what had happened, she at once collapsed in shock and then died.

Aware of the transitory nature of life on Earth, Chadanta willingly offered himself as a sacrifice to the whims of his vengeful wife. While his complicity amazed his captors, he looked forward to spiritual rebirth beyond death.

The Beneficent King

At one time, the Buddha dwelt on Earth as king of the Sibis. Beloved by all his kingdom for his grace and generosity, he was also respected beyond its borders for his virtue and his strength. The poor and hungry flocked to his palace from across the world, and all were welcomed as friends.

After some time, however, the good king looked upon his needy recipients in dismay. He realized that his giving had cost him nothing—only various material items that had no spiritual worth. So he began to wonder what it would be like to renounce something really significant—a living limb, for example, or an essential organ.

The implications of such a momentous question could not but reverberate in the heavens. The king was heard by Shakra, who wondered how he would act. Disguising himself as an old blind *brahmin*, the god made his way to the royal palace. There he joined the throng of beggars gathered to take advantage of the king's continuing largesse. As the others clamored for more trivial treasures, Shakra quietly caught the king's attention and boldly asked for the use of one of his eyes. The court gasped at the beggar's presumption, and moved to eject him, but the king stayed his guards with a wave of the hand. Delighted to be asked for what he had himself yearned to be able to offer, he insisted that the beggar take not one but both eyes. And after an agonizing operation to remove the

organs, he had them implanted in the old man's face. His courtiers were aghast and his people grief-stricken: the king's renunciation and endurance were not well understood. His wounds slowly healed, though, and his people's shock softened. The king himself was fortified by his loss and felt no regret – except on one account. No longer could he see the faces lit up by his generosity, the gratitude of those he helped.

So when one day, all of a sudden, the god Shakra appeared before him, offering him his heart's desire, he did not hesitate in his request. An eye was what he wanted, he said, so that he might see the radiant faces of those whose needs he had helped assuage. No sooner had he spoken than a beautiful eye appeared, blue as the finest lotus flower, with a precious sapphire at its heart. Exhilarated as he was by the god's great gift, the king boldly asked for a second. The Earth trembled, the mountains shook and the sea boiled and bubbled, so great was the joy in heaven and Earth as the king's sight was restored in full. Now, said Shakra, he would be able to see through any obstruction. All of the Earth for hundreds of miles around would be open to his gaze. He would be able to seek out suffering and alleviate want wherever it was hiding: his capacity to do good had been enhanced beyond his wildest dreams. Shakra disappeared, and the king was left in wonder. Divine choirs sang in gladness, while the people rejoiced with their king.

The *bodhisattva*, however, came into conflict with another king who was less virtuous. This time, reborn as a hermit, he was living deep in the forest, in a cave. Yet while he had renounced the world for his own part, it seemed to seek him out here in his

Above: This 1st–2nd-century grey schist torso, from Gandhara, Afghanistan, shows the Buddha as Prince Siddhartha. His generosity as king of the Sibis, one of his later incarnations, led him to make one of his most dramatic sacrifices.

sanctuary, for one day the king of the realm arrived, having come to this quietest of spots to play erotic games with his wives. Unoccupied once their master had fallen asleep, the women set out to explore, and they stumbled upon the hermit's hiding place. There they joined the audience of gods and men who had come to listen to the *bodhisattva's* wise words. Spellbound, they soon lost track of time, and they did not even notice when the king arrived, outraged at having been abandoned. Fiercely berating his womenfolk, he ordered them away, but the teacher remonstrated with him, counselling him to patience. Outraged that any holy man should presume to preach to him, the king retorted as he drew his sword that he would test the hermit's own patience to the fullest. With several mighty blows, he cut the *bodhisattva* into pieces. Yet throughout this bloody assault, his defenseless victim did not raise so much as a murmur. There was no protest against this agonizing fate. By the death of this Earthly body, he knew beyond doubt, a higher destiny would be served, and all who witnessed his end went away inspired to live new and better lives of their own.

Arya Sura, hidden author of the *Jatakamala*

One of the most famous collections of Jataka stories is the Jatakamala of Arya Sura. Its thirty-four stories are beautifully wrought in both verse and prose. Its origins, however, are obscure. Some scholars believe it was compiled around the fifth or sixth century CE, others that it was written earlier. But of the author, nothing certain is known at all.

Claims that Arya Sura was a king's son, a wandering ascetic or a scholar from Sri Lanka, however pleasing or plausible, are speculations of compilers writing many centuries after his death.

Yet some sense of Arya Sura's personality does emerge from his book. While his artistry is consummate, and clearly self-conscious, the moral imperative remains paramount for him. All *Jataka* stories were moral in intent and a number passed directly into Western tradition. Arya Sura's emphasis on self-sacrifice, however, marks him out from the rest of *Jataka* writers. The theme of selflessness recurs throughout the *Jatakamala*, and was clearly dear to the author's heart. Arya Sura's deep sympathy with the world also emerges in the characters he created who live and breathe with real psychological depth.

People dance and play music in a detail from the Amaravati stupa in Andhra Pradesh. This tall limestone relief, from the 1st century CE, illustrates tales from the *Jatakas* and marks what was once the holiest Buddhist site in southern India.

The Wandering Ascetic

Another existence saw the *bodhisattva* as a wandering ascetic, Bodhi. Having mastered every discipline of human art and learning, he then renounced them all to follow the path of simple piety. Yet his attempts to retreat from the world were troubled, for the world would not readily forgo his insights.

A great king asked Bodhi to stay as his guest in return for his wise instruction. The two men's friendship flourished, but others at the court became jealous and tried to force the priest out.

For a long time they were unsuccessful in their efforts, the king proving unswerving in his love. But the relentless stream of hints and insinuations wore away at his spirit, until his faith in his teacher was fatally undermined. Sensing this, Bodhi decided to take his leave.

Bodhi resumed his wanderings, replenishing his spirit among nature's woods and streams. Yet concern for his sometime student kept troubling his conscience. He knew that the king would be at the mercy of his scheming counsellors, so Bodhi came up with a plan to return and help him back to the true path. Knowing that the killing of a fellow creature could never be justified, he conjured up before him a monkey, and then magically stripped it of its skin. Stepping into it himself, he made his way back to the royal palace. In this strange animal apparel, he walked into the council chamber where the king was seated with his court. The king saluted him civilly, but wanted to know how had he come by this most extraordinary of suits. Bodhi calmly told him he had taken it from the monkey who owned it. The king's advisers could barely believe their good fortune: to have killed a living creature was a clear transgression of the law. They had caught the priest in a shameful act. Yet Bodhi effortlessly refuted their objections, tying up their minds in those same skilful sophistries that they had used to entangle the king. With their own

Complete withdrawal from worldly matters is shown by this stone figure of a fasting buddha, from Pakistan. The praying figures on the statue's base emphasize the Buddha's renunciation of food, action and the company of his fellow men.

absurdities exposed, they were left in total confusion. By the time Bodhi had finished, no one was willing to dispute his right to kill however many monkeys he pleased.

Bodhi then turned to their king. Of course he had killed no monkey, he said: he had merely conjured it. To do harm to a fellow creature could never be justified. The king should learn by this experience to give his trust only to virtue, to the simplicities of the soul that made right and wrong clear. Gentleness, generosity and fairness were the attributes of the beneficent ruler. All acknowledged the righteousness and wisdom of his words, and the king offered him his heartfelt thanks for his timely return. His work now done, however, Bodhi left the court a second time, once more to wander peacefully along the quiet byways of the world.

The King and His Good Chaplain

Not everyone appreciated the bodhisattva's holy works. He once served as a priest in the palace of King Yasapani of Benares but soon fell foul of the king's malicious adviser. Snared by the intrigue of court, he was to discover that wisdom and generosity were as often attended by jealousy and hatred as by thankfulness.

The royal adviser Kalaka resented the holy presence of the *bodhisattva*, since it highlighted his own corruption. The constant check on his own ambitions was bad enough, but the priest had recently ruled correctly and scrupulously in a case he himself had attempted to pervert. He resolved to get rid of the meddling holy man. So, whispering lies and calumnies to the king and persuading him to fear his chaplain's growing popularity among the people, Kalaka coaxed his royal master into setting a trap for the priest. He convinced the king to give him a series of impossible tasks and then put him to death when he failed to complete them. For the first test, the king ordered the *bodhisattva* to build him a pleasure garden, but allowed him only a day to complete it. The priest thus spent a sleepless night, wondering what on earth he was going to do, for he knew it would take him hundreds of days and nights to accomplish what he had to do in one. But his answer came from heaven. The god Shakra appeared by his

bedside and told him not to worry. He assured the anguished chaplain that the appointed task would be completed with the dawn. And so indeed it proved, the morning sun rising to reveal a green garden of delectable beauty and exoticism—and the king at once astounded and alarmed. Setting his chaplain a series of ever more challenging tasks, he found him easily accomplishing them all with Shakra's divine assistance—creating a beautiful lake, a pleasure palace, and a huge, dazzling jewel. The astonished king was finally forced to recognize that his chaplain enjoyed the support of the gods. It was the scheming Kalaka, he realized, who was practicing against virtue. He embraced his priest's friendship and immediately put his counsellor to death.

When Yasapani saw the magnificent wonders the humble priest had created, he soon recognized the handiwork of the gods themselves.

The Spiritual Anatomy of Jainism

Although the Jain universe is a highly complicated system of layers and divinities, it is founded in the purest simplicity. Its cosmos, maintained by an infinite succession of time-cycles, is bound by the image of a headless human body of enormous beauty and size.

Reality is many-sided for Jain theologians: no single perspective can be entirely adequate, since every individual standpoint brings a view of its own. The Jain universe, therefore, contains many contradictions, yet all are brought together in a single intricate but elegant whole. The headless body of a man provides the model for the structure of the cosmos, and it is divided into three parts: the torso, waist and legs. In the right leg, seven hells are set aside for sinners, each with a specific type of torture ready to be inflicted on the condemned.

In the left leg there is the underworld, Patala, where deities and demons dwell, all lined up in their ranks, with each order in a different kind of tree. The most dreadful of the demons are the Vana Vyantaras, but all the spirits here are devils to be feared. The man's midriff is our own world, which spreads out in concentric circles, the lofty peak of

The city of Jaisalmer, in northwest India, was founded in 1156 by the Bhati prince Jaisal. It flourished under the influence of its Jain merchants and bankers from the 14th to 16th centuries.

The Lesson of Time

Time, in Jainism, is an endlessly turning wheel, a series of cycles that rise and fall for eternity. With each revolution, the fortunes of the world reverse and the teachers of Jainism are born.

A benign serpent presides over time's upwards, Utsarpini stage, through which it moves in six ever-improving phases. Having peaked in perfection, it immediately enters its Avasarpini stage, plunging downwards through six ages of deepening degeneracy, supervised by an evil serpent. On the brink of disaster, however, time enters another upwards Utsarpini, and so the cycle continues through eternity. At each stage of each cycle, new spiritual teachers are created. Called *tirthankaras*, or "ford-builders," they are leaders who have created a path for their followers across the deep ocean of suffering that is human life. Mahavira is the most famous of these teachers; others include Rishabadeva, who attained nirvana on the top of the holy mountain, Kailasa, and Neminatha, a cousin of the Hindu god Krishna. While it has close ties to Buddhism, Jainism derived many of its deities and demons from Hinduism.

The spiritual path of Jainism is created and maintained by the 24 *tirthankaras*, or "ford-builders," two of whom are shown in this detail from a Bundi watercolor, *c.* 1720.

Mount Meru the hub on which everything turns. Eight oceans ring this mighty mountain, with eight continents between them: in these rings of existence, all mortal life is contained.

Above in the body's torso are the ascending levels of heaven. First comes Kalpa, with its sixteen celestial realms. Above that is Kalpathitha, home of the benevolent deities. They occupy Kalpathitha's fourteen levels, grouped according to their rank. Highest of all is Indra, the most potent deity in heaven and Earth.

Yet Indra's position, significantly, is not that of universal intelligence. Though king of gods and men, he is not king of the cosmos. The body of the universe is headless, without any single directing mind. No god, however powerful, is above the need for self-perfection; everyone, mortals and deities alike, can learn from the wisdom of the sage. Above the Kalpathitha, beyond the endless swirl of *karma*, is to be found the sacred realm of Siddha Sila, where only the holiest dwell. Mahavira, the great Jain teacher, lives here, along with other Siddhas, those blessed few who have attained perfection and left the life of the universe behind. But these beings cannot be regarded as rulers of the cosmos, any more than the highest gods can. They do not head the cosmic body, but instead have transcended its cycles completely and abide here in utter stillness, beyond the Earthly considerations of mortality and time.

The Life of Mahavira

The life of Mahavira, great teacher of Jainism, offers parallels with that of the Buddha, his approximate contemporary. Born a warrior prince, he later became the twenty-fourth, and most celebrated, *tirthankara* after achieving enlightenment as a wandering ascetic.

A strange series of dreams heralded Mahavira's arrival on Earth. Night after night his mother, Trisala, a noblewoman of Benares, was visited by miraculous images of unimaginable portent. First came a great white elephant, trumpeting in triumph; then came a huge bellowing bull. A roaring white lion followed, a clear symbol of kingship and strength. Then Sri Lakshmi, the goddess of good fortune, appeared to bless the life to come. It was clear by now that such important signs could only mean some momentous birth.

A child was at last born. The beautiful boy, named Vardhamana, was strong in both body and mind. He was still small when he overpowered a rogue elephant, and he proved fearless when a god one day bore him high into the air to test his

Like the Buddha, Mahavira found enlightenment as a wandering ascetic. He is shown here with his disciples, in a detail from the 13th-century Jain manuscript, the *Kalpa Sutra.*

courage. Far from struggling in terror or pleading to be set down, the child tore out his abductor's hair and freed himself by force. According to one Jain tradition, Vardhamana grew up to marry the princess Yosoda, a girl famed far and wide for her beauty and virtue. She bore him a beautiful daughter, but he left his family to wander the world. All agree that, by the age of thirty, Vardhamana had dedicated himself to prayer and poverty, roaming India's dusty highways, preaching and begging for his food. Twelve years passed in this way before he sensed the moment had come for something more. At that point, his mind purified by prayer and his body prepared by fasting, he settled down beneath a tree to await the advent of enlightenment. The gods gathered across the skies

An 18th-century Jain icon, made from brass in Rajasthan, representing the release of the spirit. Jains believe that human consciousness knows no boundaries.

to witness this most miraculous of moments. When the ecstatic instant came, they swooped from the sky and bore him off through the air, to set him up on a five-tiered throne. There they honored him and gave him the title of Mahavira, "Great Hero." All ties with the world now set firmly aside, all possessions discarded as dross, Mahavira tore off his clothes and pulled his hair out by the roots, scorning to shave his head, contemptuous as he was of pain. Some Jains say that the special white robes that he wore from this day did not count as possessions. Others insist that their founder shunned clothes and went naked.

Whatever he wore, and wherever he went, the life of Mahavira was a lesson in piety and patience. Indifferent to pain and discomfort, he heeded only the hunger of the soul. Once, provoked by this otherworldly detachment, a group of herdsmen tried to torture him into a response. But though they drove sharp nails through his ears and singed the skin of his feet with naked flames, Mahavira merely smiled, scarcely conscious in his exalted spiritual

state of the terrible agonies his body endured. On another occasion, rapt in prayer in a field, Mahavira failed to hear when the farmer asked him to keep an eye on his browsing stock while he went away for a time. When he returned, his cattle had gone, while Mahavira prayed on unaware. He did not notice the farmer's bitter complaints either, and after a while the man gave up in exasperation and went off to try and find his missing cattle himself. Returning some time later after a fruitless search, the farmer found his cattle back in their accustomed pasture, grazing quietly as if nothing had happened, the holy man praying peacefully in their midst. Convinced by now that this stranger was trying to steal his cattle, the farmer attacked him and attempted to wring his neck. He would have succeeded had the great god Indra not intervened to save Mahavira's life, since the holy man continued to pray, oblivious to the danger he was in.

At last the time came when Mahavira felt it was time for him to die, and so, summoning all the great kings and ministers of the world, he preached to them for seven full days, giving them all the benefit of his wisdom. He sketched out the philosophy of Jainism and its central ethic of nonviolence; he mapped out its metaphysics and explained the workings of its universe. Finally, on the seventh day, he mounted a vast diamond throne that shimmered in the starlight. A deep sleep came over his listeners, and all the lights of the universe were dimmed. Waking into darkness, Mahavira's followers lit torches. Their teacher had vanished, his soul finally liberated in death. A Siddha now, he had perfected his soul, and escaped the endless cycle of karmic reincarnation. But even if the great teacher was finally dead, his wisdom would live on in the form of an enduring religion of gentleness and peace.

133

THE LEGACY OF INDIAN MYTH

Despite modernization and economic change, Asian lifestyles remain strongly spiritual. Buddhist altars nestle among Bangkok's skyscrapers, and Bombay businessmen make offerings to Lakshmi. And the great sagas of the *Ramayana* and *Mahabharata* are still eagerly recited, not just in India but in Java, Bali, Thailand and beyond.

The major legacy of the post-Vedic age is probably the story of Rama itself. There have always been, and continue to be, countless departures from the classical Sanskrit rendition, composed around 300 BCE by the poet Valmiki. India's spirited oral tradition to this day produces highly localized variations of the poem that address the particular problems of a place or period.

India's women, notably, have made various adjustments to Valmiki's version, written down by a man and dominated by male characters and perspectives. For example, Santa, Rama's older sister, hardly appears in the "official" version, but in a Telugu *Ramayana* she becomes a major character. This reflects Santa's importance as a regional deity in Andhra Pradesh, and it is also an assertion of female power: as the big sister, Santa takes every opportunity to command, reprimand and discipline Rama. The growing Hindu diaspora could yet add Western nuances to the story, giving new levels of meaning to this most versatile of legends.

Religion also mixes with politics in India and continues to shape government attitudes and strategy. India is a secular state, but given the interweaving of religion and everyday life, it would be a rash parliamentary candidate who failed to take account of Hindu issues. Religion, and the old legends, are regularly (if not always successfully) invoked to secure electoral advantage.

The legends also serve as symbols of conflict. E. V. Ramaswami Naiker, the Tamil separatist leader, had political objections to the *Ramayana's* underlying theme of north conquering south. He wanted to reassert local Dravidian traditions in the face of what he saw as Brahmanical Hindu northern domination. In 1922 he asked his followers to burn the *Ramayana*. He then published an alternative reading, lampooning Sita as a gold-digger, Hanuman as an arsonist and murderer and Lakshmana as a lecherous sadist. When the Uttar Pradesh government banned the book, he arranged for his satirical play, the *Keemayana* (*keema* is a nonsense sound)—featuring a drunk Rama and a slovenly Sita—to tour Tamil Nadu.

The climax to Ramaswami's campaign came in 1956, when he tried to hold a mass public burning of pictures of Rama—a reversal of the northern tradition of incinerating images of Ravana, the villain of the *Ramayana*. Hundreds of people showed up clutching boxes of matches and pictures torn out of magazines, but the demonstration was called off after police arrested Ramaswami. Today's rebels, from Kashmir to Sri Lanka, may not wield the same theological weapons as Ramaswami, but they often fight in the names of Durga and Kali, the bloodthirsty, human-flesh-devouring goddesses of death and destruction.

The Impact of Television

It says much for the continuing vitality and influence of Hindu myth that it has also drawn India's biggest-ever television audiences. In 1987–1988, Doordarshan, the government-run TV network, serialized the *Ramayana* in fifty-two forty-five-minute episodes. Critical broadsides were swept away by a tidal wave of popular support. At 9:30 every Sunday morning, when the series was screened, the subcontinent ground to a halt as 800 million people settled down to watch.

Far from turning the great epic into cheap soap opera, the serial transformed television sets into religious artifacts. An important part of Hindu worship is *darshan* (sighting)—the act of seeing images of the gods and epic characters in temples and shrines. The video *Ramayana* was a banquet of *darshan*, with the legendary characters moving, speaking and interacting as never before. Viewers purified themselves by ritual bathing before the show and garlanded their sets with flowers and decorations, setting them on altars consecrated with Ganges water and goat dung. Streets were hung with pennants as Rama's enthronement approached and, when the episode was finally shown, viewers celebrated by blowing horns, ringing bells and setting off fireworks.

Doordarshan's *Ramayana* highlighted India's complex filigree of society, literature and legend in a wholly unexpected way. Ramanand Sagar, who produced and directed the series, followed Tulsidas's Hindi version, which concludes with Rama ascending to the throne and the start of an age of idyllic peace. Pressure mounted on Sagar to produce more episodes, based on Valmiki's longer version—in which Rama eventually banishes Sita. Because Valmiki is widely believed to have come from a low-caste family, he commands great loyalty from northern India's lowest castes, among them the sanitary workers. Sagar's preference for Tulsidas angered them so much that they went on strike. Rubbish accumulated rapidly, a cholera epidemic loomed and within days Sagar was served with a court order commanding him to extend the series. Assured that more programs would be made, the workers went back to work; in the end, the series extended to seventy-eight episodes.

The televised *Ramayana* was the latest development in a rich tradition of storytelling. Newspapers dubbed director Sagar "the Tulsidas of the video age," and when the series was repackaged in video format, he personally introduced each episode in the manner of a Hindu sage. Labels on the tapes themselves, packaged lavishly like idols, warned that it was not only a crime but a sin to make pirated copies of such a sacred text.

Sagar's immediate predecessors were filmmakers. India's pioneer of cinema, Dadasaheb Phalke, dramatized the burning of Lanka (1917) and the birth of Krishna (1919). When the films toured agricultural communities, audiences prostrated themselves before the screen whenever lord Rama appeared. The only films Gandhi liked were

The televised version of the *Ramayana* was so popular that a series dramatizing the *Mahabharata* was soon commissioned. In this scene, the Kauravas try to undress Pandu's wife Draupadi, played here by Malika Sarabhai. Krishna, however, comes to the rescue and no matter how many layers of Draupadi's clothes they pull off, she remains clothed.

A group of Hindus meet to read and discuss holy books. *Katha*, the practice of narrating sacred texts, is an ancient tradition but one that remains central to the Hindu faith. Instead of including the ritual observances necessary at a church, temple or shrine, these gatherings remain informal in structure, but serious in content.

Vijay Bhatt's classic *Ram Rajya* (1943) and the 1961 box-office smash *Sampoorna Ramayana* by Homi Wadia. In 1975, a movie focusing on the obscure goddess Santoshi Ma catapulted her to fame, and she is now the focus of many cults.

Filmmakers and television directors alike were using their respective media to uphold the ancient tradition of *katha* (narration). This involves either reciting the entire *Ramayana* in daily episodes, or taking a particular section of the poem and expounding on it at length.

Such continuity is also a feature of India's music scene. An unexpected hit of the 1970s was a seven-disc recording of Tulsidas's *Ramayana* by the popular singer Mukesh—still a favorite choice for background music at weddings and other functions. It was the first time that *bhajan* (devotional singing) had achieved any real commercial success. Since then *bhajan* has proved that it, too, can move with the times, and it has transferred easily from temple and stage to commercial pop.

The new *bhajans* are simplified, polished versions of ancient songs, accompanied by lush orchestration and the stylish presentation techniques of the modern music industry. In the West, these tunes might be termed "crossover" music, because they are at the same time devotional music and easy listening.

Developments in Hinduism

India's religions have evolved constantly, through the influence of other cultures or the inspiration of individuals. But as two recent Indian sects show, they all retain the essential tenets of Hinduism. According to many observers, the first of the Neo-Hindus was Sahajanand Swami (1781–1830), who founded a *sampradaya* (a tradition, school or fellowship) in early nineteenth-century Gujarat. Today he has many followers, and temples dedicated to him contain idols in his clothes and with his moustachioed face. To traditional scriptures like the *Bhagavad Gita*, the Swaminarayan religion has added its own text, the *Vachanamritam*.

Another development is that of the Brahma Kumari (Daughters of Brahma), a millenarian movement founded in the late 1930s by a Sindhi businessman, Dada Lekhraj. After experiencing a series of visions, Lekhraj prophesied the imminent end of the world, which only a small, pure elite would survive. The energetic proselytizing of the Brahma Kumaris has been condemned by mainstream Hindus, and their idea that women are capable of sanctity is considered a dangerous innovation. Their advocacy of celibacy has been criticized as an unacceptably radical statement of independence for women.

India's religions have also felt the influence of Western values, and as Indian emigrants become more settled in countries such as the USA, Canada and the United Kingdom, religious traditions are facing new challenges. In Britain, weddings have been adapted to fit the local legal requirements. Similarly, Hindu burial and mourning procedures have evolved to address the practicalities of dealing with British housing, crematoria and funeral directors. The future for Indian traditions abroad, as in India, lies in flexibility.

Meanwhile, the impact of Indian culture on the West is ever-growing. The popularity of Indian cuisine and the familiar sound of the sitar and tabla have opened the door to a much wider set of traditionally Hindu and Jain values. Gandhi's philosophy of nonviolent resistance has transferred effortlessly to Western protest: one of the key principles of Greenpeace, for example, is "non-violent direct action." For decades, yoga has been practiced by millions in the West who speak warmly of its benefits, although many have no idea that the first *yogis* lived in the third millennium BCE, predating even the Aryan invasions. Meditation—as preached by the Beatles' guru, Mahesh Yogi, in the 1960s and 1970s—helps stressed Westerners to lower their blood pressure without drugs.

The prominence of Indian beliefs in today's alternative lifestyles is proof of their undying, versatile appeal. Hinduism is timeless, its past, present and future bound by an enduring spiritual tradition. It is therefore impossible to speak of a legacy, especially as India's rituals and beliefs are still thriving, constantly evolving yet always the same.

Shantilal Soni's *Rambhakt Hanuman*, produced in 1969, takes as its hero Hanuman, the great monkey general of the *Ramayana*. This was one of many Indian films that drew on the Hindu epics, which proved as fruitful a source of cinematic superheroes as ancient Greece had been for Hollywood in the 1950s.

137

Glossary

amrita The intoxicating food of the gods, also known as *soma*.

asura The most common name for a demon.

atman The manifestation of *brahman*, or the divine principle, in the human soul, the Self.

bhakti The practice of religious devotion.

bodhisattva One who is capable of nirvana but delays attaining it through compassion with those bound by mortal suffering.

brahman The supreme, all-permeating divine reality or absolute truth.

brahmins Hindu priests who occupied the highest rank of the caste system.

darshan The experience of the divine through seeing, and being seen by, the image of god.

dharma The eternal law of the cosmos; right and moral behavior.

dhyana Contemplation, deep meditation.

jati Caste or social division.

karma The cycle of causality; the belief that deeds, in this or previous lives, decide destiny.

kshatriya The warrior caste, second only in superiority to the *brahmins*.

lingam The phallus, or male sex organ, often worshipped as an image of the god Shiva.

mantra A holy formula that is chanted in order to summon a god.

mokshadvara A door to liberation, through which one is released from the eternal cycle of birth, death and rebirth, or *samsara*.

nirvana The ultimate state of consciousness, also interpreted as heaven.

Om The sacred syllable from which the gods and all matter, were made. Also denotes Shiva.

samhitas Songs of praise exalting the gods found in the *Rig Veda*.

samsara The cycle of birth, death and rebirth.

shakti The essence of female energy.

soma Alternative name for *amrita*, the intoxicating food of the gods.

tapas Heat or energy derived from meditation and austerities.

tirthankara A "ford-builder"; one of twenty-four Jain leaders who create a way across the sea of human suffering for their followers.

trimurti The triad, or trinity, of Hinduism, which includes Brahma, Vishnu and Shiva.

vidya A process of unitary thought that sees everything as linked: God and Man, spirit and matter.

yoni The symbol of female energy.

For More Information

Asian Art Museum
200 Larkin Street
San Francisco, CA 94102
(415) 581-3500
Web site: http://www.asianart.org
The Asian Art Museum of San Francisco is one of the largest museums in the Western world devoted exclusively to Asian art, with a collection of over 17,000 artworks spanning 6,000 years of history.

The British Museum
Great Russell Street
London WC1B 3DG
United Kingdom
+44 (0)20 7323 8299
Web site: http://www.britishmuseum.org
South Asia is the seat of many of the world's great religious traditions, including Buddhism, Hinduism and Jainism. Objects in the British Museum collection explore the central beliefs of these faiths and their development from the early centuries CE to modern times.

Freer Gallery of Art / Arthur M. Sackler Gallery
Smithsonian Institution
1050 Independence Ave. SW
P.O. Box 37012, MRC 707
Washington, DC 20013-7012
(202) 633-1000
Web site: http://www.asia.si.edu
The Freer Gallery of Art and the Arthur M. Sackler Gallery are two Smithsonian museums that aim to present the best in Asian art while enabling visitors to walk through a vivid timeline of world cultures.

The Metropolitan Museum of Art
1000 Fifth Avenue
New York, NY 10028-0198
(212) 535-7710
Web site: http://www.metmuseum.org
Galleries within the museum present the visual traditions of South and Southeast Asia, including India, from the earliest civilizations to the sixteenth century. Museum resources explore the imagery and symbolism associated with Hindu and Buddhist deities in South Asian art.

Rubin Museum of Art
150 West 17th Street
New York, NY 10011
(212) 620-5000
Web site: http://www.rmanyc.org
The Rubin Museum of Art is a nonprofit cultural and educational institution dedicated to the collection, display, and preservation of the art of the Himalayas. It boasts the largest Western collection of religious art from the cultures of this region.

Web Sites

Due to the changing nature of Internet links, Rosen Publishing has developed an online list of Web sites related to the subject of this book. This site is updated regularly. Please use this link to access the list:

http://www.rosenlinks.com/wmyth/inda

For Further Reading

Bechert, Heinz, and Richard Gombrich. (eds.) *The World of Buddhism*. Thames and Hudson: London, 1984.

Carrithers, Michael. *The Buddha*. Oxford University Press: Oxford, 1984.

Easwaran, Eknath. (trans.) *The Bhagavad Gita*. Arkana/Penguin: London, 1985.

Easwaran, Eknath. (trans.) *The Dhammapada*. Penguin: London, 1986.

Easwaran, Eknath. (trans.) *The Upanishads*. Arkana/Penguin: London, 1987.

Flood, Gavin. *An Introduction to Hinduism*. Cambridge University Press: Cambridge, 1996.

Griffin, Ralph T.H. (trans.) *The Rig Veda*. Forgotten Books: Charleston, California, 2008.

Hartsuiker, Dolf. *Sadhus, Holy Men of India*. Thames and Hudson: London, 1993.

Jaffrey, Madhur. *Seasons of Splendour: Tales, Myths and Legends of India*. Puffin: London, 1985.

Jansen, Eva Rudy. *The Book of Hindu Imagery*. Binkey Kok Publications: Holland, 1993.

Kapur, Kamla K. *Ganesha Goes to Lunch*. Mandala Publishing: San Rafael, California, 2007.

Long, Jeffrey D. *Jainism: An Introduction*. I. B. Tauris: London, 2009.

Mackenzie, Donald A. *Indian Myth and Legend*. The Gresham Publishing Company: London, 1913.

Mookerjee, Ajit. *Kali, The Feminine Force*. Thames and Hudson: London, 1988.

Pauling, Chris. *Introducing Buddhism*. Windhorse Publications: Birmingham, 1990.

Shearer, Alistair. *The Hindu Vision*. Thames and Hudson: London, 1993.

Index

Page numbers in *italic* denote captions. Where there is a textual reference to the topic on the same page as a caption, italics have not been used.